T
BLACK BOOK OF

NEW YORK

*The Essential Guide to the
Quintessential City*

BEN GIBBERD

ILLUSTRATED BY KERREN BARBAS

PETER PAUPER PRESS, INC.
WHITE PLAINS, NEW YORK

FOR NINA AND JACK,
TRUE NEW YORKERS

*The editors would like to extend a special
thanks to cartographer David Lindroth
for his tireless efforts on this project*

Designed by Heather Zschock

Illustrations copyright © 2006 Kerren Barbas

The Map is copyrighted by the MTA. Used by permission.
Neighborhood maps © 2006 David Lindroth Inc.

Copyright © 2006
Peter Pauper Press, Inc.
202 Mamaroneck Avenue
White Plains, NY 10601
All rights reserved
ISBN 1-59359-932-3
Printed in Hong Kong
7 6 5 4 3 2 1

Visit us at www.peterpauper.com

THE LITTLE
BLACK BOOK OF
NEW YORK

CONTENTS

INTRODUCTION

New York City is immense, the biggest city in the United States and one of the biggest in the world, with a population of nearly 8 million covering 321 square miles. It's packed with some of the most famous restaurants, museums, buildings, and visitor sites in the world. Our pocket-sized *Little Black Book of New York* covers the top picks for each neighborhood, in an easy-to-use and un-intimidating format for those new to the city. You can take this book with you anywhere in Manhattan—knowing it will provide a succinct list of what's essential in every neighborhood, from art galleries to architecture—and because of its size, most people won't even know you're a tourist!

We've broken Manhattan down by neighborhoods, and then grouped adjoining neighborhoods into eight individual maps and chapters for convenience; and there's also a public transportation map at the back. If you'd rather look things up by their specific names, we've included an index, too. We hope you enjoy your visit, and that you'll find all you need in this Little Black Book to navigate this great city with pleasure and aplomb.

NEW YORK STREET GRID

New York is a pretty easy city to get around, thanks to its grid plan that was adopted in 1811. The plan called for 12 numbered avenues running north and south roughly parallel to the Hudson River, and about 155 cross streets running east and west. Exceptions to this plan include Broadway, which was in place at the time of the 1811 plan. It cuts an angle from southeast to northwest. Rather than change it, this was turned to the city's advantage by creating "squares" wherever Broadway crossed a north-south avenue. The famed Broadway is now practically synonymous with New York City. Greenwich Village (below 14th Street) was also able to keep its confusing street pattern (largely because it had been kept separate from the rest of the city by a yellow fever and cholera epidemic in the early 1800s). The streets of the Village are for the most part the same as they were in the early 1800s, with crooked paths best suited for walking. The winding roads can make this area a bit challenging to navigate, but the charming cobblestone streets are well worth it.

HOW TO USE THIS GUIDE

We have included eight fold-out maps, by neighbor-hood sections, with color-coded keys to help you find the places listed in the text. **Red** symbols indicate **Places to See**, which include land-marks, arts & entertainment, and fun stuff to do with kids. **Blue** symbols indicate **Places to Eat & Drink**, which include restaurants, bars, and nightlife. Orange symbols indicate Where to Shop. And Green symbols indicate Where to Stay.

Here are our keys for restaurant and hotel costs:

Restaurants
Cost of an appetizer and main course without drinks
($)   Up to $25
($$) $25-$45
($$$) $45 and up

Hotels
Cost per night
($) $50-$125
($$) $125-$250
($$$) $250 and up

PUBLIC TRANSPORTATION

The public transportation map at the back lets you
know how to get around fast and easily on the subways.
We've started each neighborhood section with a listing
of which subways (and subway stops) to use to get to the
neighborhood.

A free copy of the subway map is available at any subway station booth. The main way to pay for public
transportation is the MetroCard®, a magnetic fare card,
which is sold at all subway station booths, and through
vending machines (that accept cash, debit, and credit
cards) that are in many subway stations, and at many
other locations. You can use a MetroCard at all subway
stations and on all public and many private buses with-
in New York City. If you use a MetroCard, you can

transfer free of charge between subway and bus, bus and subway, bus and bus. One-Day Fun Pass and seven- to 30-day unlimited ride MetroCards are also available.

SUBWAY TIPS

Listen Up
As with any mass public transportation system, there are bound to be service changes, repairs, interruptions, etc. Don't panic! Just listen to the conductors for their specific directions, read the signs posted, and don't be afraid to ask other passengers questions. New Yorkers (contrary to their bad rap) are helpful and love to dispense directions to show off their New York knowledge.

Downtown-Uptown
When you're entering a subway station, pay attention to whether you're using the "Downtown" entrance or the "Uptown" entrance. They're usually right across the street from each other. You don't want to end up paying twice because you went through the wrong entrance! Some of the bigger stations don't split their entrances on the street level (for example, Times Square). In those cases, you can choose the uptown or downtown side once you get underground.

chapter 1

FINANCIAL DISTRICT
BATTERY PARK CITY
TRIBECA
CIVIC CENTER

FINANCIAL DISTRICT
BATTERY PARK CITY
TRIBECA
CIVIC CENTER

Places to See:
1. Wall Street
2. Trinity Church
3. New York Stock Exchange
4. St. Paul's Chapel
5. Ground Zero
6. Bowling Green
7. Battery Park/Ferries
8. Wall Street Bull
9. National Museum of the American Indian
10. New York City Police Museum
11. South Street Seaport Museum
12. Fraunces Tavern Museum
20. Staten Island Ferry/Whitehall Ferry Terminal
25. Waterfront
26. North Cove Yacht Harbor
27. Winter Garden/World Financial Center
28. Museum of Jewish Heritage
29. Esplanade
30. Rockefeller Park
31. Robert F. Wagner, Jr. Park
34. Duane Park
35. New York Mercantile Exchange Building
36. Knitting Factory
37. Soho Photo Gallery
38. Tribeca Performing Arts Center
56. City Hall
57. Municipal Building
58. Woolworth Building

Places to Eat & Drink:
13. McDonald's
14. Coast
15. Delmonico's
16. Heartland Brewery & Beer Hall
17. Carmine's Italian Seafood Restaurant
18. The Full Shilling
19. Fino Wall St. Ristorante
32. Terry's Deli
33. Lili's Noodle Shop
39. Edward's
40. Chanterelle

Chicago, Boston, Detroit,
they're all the same,
except New York…
that is a city!

—*Eve Minard, in* For Me and My Gal *(1942)*

FINANCIAL DISTRICT

④⑤ to Wall St.; ②③ to Wall St.

◦ SNAPSHOT ◦

Manhattan Island was settled by Europeans, moving south to north, so the oldest neighborhoods are here in what is called Lower Manhattan. At the southern tip is Battery Park, one of New York's oldest public open spaces. More than four million people annually visit the park and its major landmark, Castle Clinton National Monument. Wall Street—so named for the defensive wall that stood here when this area was a Dutch town in the 1600s—and the adjacent financial center are now the financial hub of New York. Although this area has become increasingly residential, with more bars, restaurants, and other amenities than ever before, it's still mostly thought of as a place to work.

PLACES TO SEE
Landmarks:

Wall Street (1) runs east of Broadway to South Street, and was originally a wooden wall built by the Dutch marking the city's northernmost edge. Although the city's financial institutions are now spread over a much wider area (especially post 9/11), this district is still the epicenter of the country's finances. Walking west, check out **Trinity Church (2)** *(Broadway/Wall Sts., 212-602-0800, admission free)*, a beautiful Gothic Revival structure that offers lunchtime concerts *(see www.trinitywallstreet.org for concert details and opening times)*, with its adjacent churchyard where such notables as Alexander Hamilton are buried. The arch temple to Mammon with its columned portico, the **New York Stock Exchange (3)** *(11 Wall Street, Broad/New Sts.)* unfortunately has been closed to the public since 9/11. Other nearby landmarks are the lovely 18th-century **St. Paul's Chapel (4)** *(209 Broadway, Fulton/Vesey Sts.)*, which houses George Washington's original pew, and, of course, **Ground Zero (5)** *(Liberty/ Vesey Sts., west of Church St.)*, sad former site of the World Trade Center towers. Beware the plethora of street vendors peddling 9/11 kitsch. Further south are two oases of green amid the canyons, tiny **Bowling Green (6)** at the foot of Broadway and **Battery Park (7)** *(south of Battery Place)*, where the **ferries (7)** to Ellis Island and the Statue of Liberty depart *(see "Arts & Entertainment," page 15)*.

Arts & Entertainment:

At **Bowling Green (6)**, you'll find the famous bronze statue of the **Wall Street Bull (8)**. Also at Bowling Green is the **National Museum of the American Indian (9)** *(1 Bowling Green, State/Whitehall Sts., 212-514-3700, www.nmai.si.edu, free admission)*, housed in the Beaux Arts former U.S. Custom House Building. The collec-

tion features thousands of works from textiles to carved stone heads. And the building itself, with its painted ceilings and great atrium, is worth the visit alone. The **New York City Police Museum (10)** *(100 Old Slip, Water/South Sts., 212-480-3100, www.nycpolicemuseum.org)*, with its re-created crime scenes complete with chalk body outlines and fake drug stashes, is more than a little hokey, but it's also one of the city's most charming and fascinating small museums. Take a **ferry** from **Battery Park (7)**: Buy ferry tickets to **Ellis Island** *(www.ellisisland.org)*, with its wonderful immigration museum, or the **Statue of Liberty** *(www.statueoflibertyferry.com)* on Liberty Island, both from Castle Clinton National Monument, a circular sandstone fort in Battery Park *(for advance tickets call 866-782-8834)*. You can also take the free **Staten Island Ferry (20)**—the city's best bargain—to Staten Island and back from the brand-new glass **Whitehall Ferry Terminal (20)** *(end of Whitehall St. at the water, 718-815-BOAT, www.siferry.com)*. The **South Street Seaport Museum (11)** *(Visitors' Center: 12 Fulton St. at South St., 212-748-8600, www.southstseaport.org)* has a great collection of old sailing ships lining the dock, offering tours

inside, plus a museum with frequently changing exhibits. The **Fraunces Tavern Museum (12)** *(54 Pearl St. corner of Broad St., 212-425-1778, www. frauncestavern museum.org)* opened to the public in 1907. The original tavern was a meeting ground for the Sons of Liberty in the pre-revolutionary years, and became the site in which Washington gave his farewell speech at the end of the war.

Kids:

The **South Street Seaport Museum (11)** has programs for kids and families. Check out "Family Fun" on its Web site, www.southstseaport.org, for details. Amid the cobblestone streets of the seaport, there's also plenty of street performers drawing crowds and needing young volunteers for spectacular stunts and magic tricks. Take your kids on a ferry to see "Lady Liberty" up close. *[Buy tickets at Castle Clinton in* **Battery Park (7).***]* And if you have young aspiring crime fighters in your family, they'll enjoy the **New York City Police Museum (10)** *(see "Arts & Entertainment," page 15).*

PLACES TO EAT & DRINK
Where to Eat:

McDonald's (13) ($) *(160 Broadway, just north of Wall St., 212-385-2063).* Yes, McDonald's. Befitting its tony locale, this one has a doorman, pianist, and waitress service. **Coast (14) ($$)** *(110 Liberty St. at Church St., 212-962-0136, www.freshshorecoast.com)* has great seafood in a simple setting right opposite Ground Zero. The cheap drinks are a plus. **Delmonico's (15) ($$$)** *(56 Beaver St. at South William St., 212-509-1144, www. delmonicosny.com)* offers classic American fare in a classic 19th-century building. **Heartland Brewery & Beer Hall (16) ($$)** *(93 South St. at Fulton St., 646-572-2337, www.heartlandbrewery.com)* is a mini-chain that's good for beers 'n' burgers basics in a nice corner space. **Carmine's Italian Seafood Restaurant (17) ($$)** *(140 Beekman St. at Front St., 212-962-8606)* is a real slice of old New York. This former Mafia hangout just yards from the bustling seaport has been in operation for more than 100 years, yet is unknown to most tourists. Enjoy fresh seafood and drinks at its ancient bar and battered wooden booths. The calamari's great.

Bars & Nightlife:

The Full Shilling (18) *(160 Pearl St., Wall/Pine Sts., 212-422-3855)* is worth going to for the décor alone—a genuine-imported-from-Ireland antique bar that puts any patron in a drinking frame of mind. There's a good selection of beers and comfort food, too. **Fino Wall St. Ristorante (19)** *(1 Wall St. at Pearl St., 212-825-1924)* is about eating as much as drinking, with its excellent Northern Italian fare and wide range of Italian wines.

WHERE TO SHOP

Don't miss Century 21 (21) *(22 Cortlandt St., Broadway/Church St., 212-227-9092, www.c21stores.com)*, a department store stuffed with designer clothes for kids and adults at low prices. There's also plenty of shopping at and around the South Street Seaport (22) *(Pier 17 and environs, South Street to the East River, Fletcher/Beekman Sts., www.southstseaport.org)*, from the Body Shop and Ann Taylor to gadget store Sharper Image. Here are some good, if touristy, places to eat and drink with some of the best views of the East River and the Brooklyn Bridge.

WHERE TO STAY

The Wall Street Inn (23) ($$-$$$) *(9 South William St. at Broad St., 212-747-1500)* is a stylish if fairly basic hotel (there's no room service) in a neighborhood otherwise given over to efficient but soulless corporate hospitality.

BATTERY PARK CITY

1 *to Chambers St., Rector St.;* **2** **3** *to Chambers St.*

SNAPSHOT

Along the Hudson River and west of the financial district is Battery Park City, a brand new mini-metropolis built on landfill that, in typical New York fashion, nestles right next to the most historic part of the city. The Esplanade is one of the star attractions of Battery Park City. Its wide pathways give pedestrians key access to the river. In the midst of this residential neighborhood lies its commercial side: the World Financial Center and Winter Garden.

PLACES TO SEE
Landmarks:

The best thing about Battery Park City (east of the Hudson River from Battery Place to Chambers St.) is its wonderful **waterfront (25)**, part of a Hudson River Greenway that runs as far north as Harlem. There are spaces to jog, walk, rollerblade, or just sit back and relax, all with amazing views of Jersey City's towers across the water. During warmer months there are always free cul-

tural events *(see www.batteryparkcity.org for details)*. The yachts moored in the **North Cove Yacht Harbor (26)** *(waterfront between Vesey/Liberty Sts.)* are worth ogling. The **Winter Garden (27)** is a glorious 10-story glass atrium with palm trees, food courts, and shopping, plus views of the Hudson and Jersey shores. It is located in the **World Financial Center (27)** plaza *(see "Where to Shop," page 21)*, which has numerous restaurants and shops, and hosts many (often free) musical and other events *(see www.worldfinancialcenter. com for details)*.

Arts & Entertainment:

The ziggurat-shaped **Museum of Jewish Heritage (28)** *(Robert F. Wagner, Jr. Park, 36 Battery Pl. at First Pl., 646-437-4200, www.mjhnyc.org)*, located in the southern end of Battery Park City, is a relative newcomer, but well worth the visit. It's packed with photographs and objects documenting the past 100 years of Jewish life, and is also a living memorial to the Holocaust. The surrounding park and nearby landscaped walkways make for a lovely outside stroll.

Kids:

Battery Park City is one of the most child-friendly places in the city, and is so well-designed that adults can enjoy it equally—something that can't be said about a lot of children's attractions. The big draw here is the beautiful 1.2-mile **Esplanade (29)** that runs along the Hudson River from Chambers Street to Battery Place and offers amazing views of the Statue of Liberty, Ellis Island, and the Jersey City waterfront. Along the Esplanade are numerous small parks for children, adults, and even dogs. For toddlers, the best one is the **Rockefeller Park (30)** *(near Chambers St.)*, which contains the Real World Sculpture Garden, filled with wonderful little bronze sculptures by artist Tom Otterness. There's also a wading fountain to cool off on those hot NYC summer days. The **Robert F. Wagner, Jr. Park (31)** *(southern tip of Battery Park City, south of the Museum of Jewish Heritage)* is also particularly good for young children. It has clean, safe bathrooms, sprinklers in the summer, water tables, and more.

PLACES TO EAT & DRINK
Where to Eat:

Battery Park City is not exactly the most renowned place for eating out, to put it mildly, though there are a number of restaurants both inside the Winter Garden atrium and lining the plaza outside (which offer amazing views over the Hudson River). If you're strolling around, your best bet is to try a couple of locals' favorites for take-out. **Terry's Deli (32) ($)** *(410 W. Chambers St. at North End Avenue, 212-267-2816)* has good, if basic, sandwiches and the like, and **Lili's Noodle Shop (33) ($)** *(102 North End Avenue near Vesey St., 212-786-1300)* offers great egg rolls.

WHERE TO SHOP

The **World Financial Center (27)** has a host of stores and specialty shops to suit all of your needs—from fine cigars to chocolates to designer clothes for men and women.

WHERE TO STAY

The **New York Marriott Financial Center (24)** ($$-$$$) *(85 West St., Albany/Carlisle Sts., 212-385-4900, www.nyc marriottfinancial.com)* comes with all the bells and whistles you'd expect, including a fancy restaurant, Internet access in each room, and fancy harbor views.

TRIBECA

❶ to Canal St., Franklin St. or Chambers St.; ❷❸ to Chambers St.; Ⓐ Ⓒ Ⓔ to Canal St.

● SNAPSHOT ●

Tribeca used to be the site of Washington Market, a major distribution center for meat, produce, and dairy products. The warehouses and store-and-loft buildings

 here date from the 19th and early 20th centuries. After the market moved to the Bronx, the neighborhood was slowly transformed into a residential one. It now offers some of the best eating, drinking, and architecture in the city.

PLACES TO SEE
Landmarks:

Tribeca is home to some of the most flamboyant creations in stone and brick, each vying to outdo the other. **Duane Park (34)** *(Hudson, Duane, and Staple Sts.)* is a delightful triangular pocket, surrounded by cast-iron buildings that were still home to remnants of the city's dairy produce industry until the late 1970s. The **New York Mercantile Exchange Building (35)** *(6 Harrison Street, Greenwich/Hudson Sts.)* has a fantastic red brick façade, complete with clock face. Once home to the dairy trade's equivalent of the stock exchange, it has been handsomely restored.

Arts & Entertainment:

Tribeca has also become famous in recent years for resident Robert DeNiro's annual **Tribeca Film Festival** *(www.tribecafilmfestival.org for details)*, held in various neighborhood locations at the end of April. Some think it has become too mainstream in recent years (more than 300,000 people attended last year), but if you're into star-gazing, then this is the place to be each spring. The **Knitting Factory (36)** *(74 Leonard St., Broadway/Church St., 212-219-3132, www.knittingfactory.com)* is one of New York's most eclectic night spots. There are three stages in this intimate venue, each hosting different musical forms every night, from indie rock to avant-garde jazz. The **Soho Photo Gallery (37)** *(15 White St., West Broadway/Church St., 212-226-8571, www.sohophoto.com)* is one of the numerous galleries that dot Tribeca. Established in 1971 as a non-profit run by a large number of photographers, it offers a dozen or so different shows a year. The Soho name remains but the gallery relocated to Tribeca in 1979.

Kids:

From October to June the **Tribeca Performing Arts Center (38)** *(199 Chambers St., Greenwich St./West Side Highway, 212-220-1460, www.tribecapac.org)* offers a mixed bag of puppet, theater, and musical shows for children aged 3 and up. If you want to eat out with your children, **Edward's (39) ($)** *(136 West Broadway, Thomas/Duane Sts., 212-233-6436, www.edwardsnyc.com)* offers a handy combination of hip interior for Mom and Dad plus child-friendly waitstaff who can serve up special kids' menu items of fish sticks and the like.

PLACES TO EAT & DRINK
Where to Eat:

Tribeca has some of the most famous restaurants in the city, and you'd be well advised to call in advance to get a table at some of them. For top-end French dining there's **Chanterelle (40) ($$$)** *(2 Harrison St. at Hudson St., 212-966-6960, www.chanterellenyc.com)*, whose elegant patrons arrive by limo. If you like Japanese food, try **Nobu (41) ($$$)** *(105 Hudson St. at Franklin St., 212-219-0500, www.myriadrestaurantgroup.com)*, chef Nobu Matsuhisa's temple to fish where, if you're lucky enough to get in, you will undoubtedly encounter some of the best people-watching in the city. It isn't hip, but if you want a quiet supper with that special someone in an elegant, high-ceilinged space where you can hear yourself talk, **Capsouto Frères (42) ($$)** *(451 Washington St., Desbrosses/Watts Sts., 212-966-4900, www.capsoutofreres.com)* is the place to go. The food is French-American,

and one of the Capsouto brothers will probably drop by your table. The restaurant is in a beautiful brick and stone building that was once a warehouse. For much more casual lunches and dinners, there's always that reliable old standard **Odeon (43) ($$)** *(145 West Broadway at Duane St., 212-233-0507, www.theodeonrestaurant.com)*, a French bistro whose fries and warm mahogany paneling combine for a dining experience as soothing as a warm bath. If you're more into a casual brunch or snack-and-run, there's **Bubby's (44) ($$)** *(120 Hudson St. at N. Moore St., 212-219-0666, www. bubbys.com)*, a corner joint that has grown into an institution and is packed on weekends.

Bars & Nightlife:

If you want something a little upmarket, Tribeca is the home of the sophisticated watering hole. **Luca Lounge Cucina (45)** *(134 Reade St., Greenwich/Hudson Sts., 212-226-8928)* is all about fine décor, antiques, a roaring fireplace in the winter, and a good glass of wine. Very romantic. **Lush Lounge (46)** *(110 Duane St., Broadway/Church St., 212-766-1275)* has—alas—a "V.I.P. suite," but don't let that put you off. For a posh and expensive place like this it's really quite friendly, and it's nice to be comfortable for once in a bar instead of perching on some chic, yet numbing, piece of architectonic furniture. **Walker's (47)** *(16 N. Moore St. at Varick St., 212-941-0142)* is a dying breed in this neighborhood—a classic, old-time bar where you can sip pints and chat in a friendly, utterly unpretentious atmosphere, and if you get hungry pop around to its long back room for above-average burgers, fries, and the like.

WHERE TO SHOP

If Deco is your thing, Antiquaria Tribeca (48) *(129 Duane St., West Broadway/Church Sts., 212-227-7500)* has tons of it, as well as other 20th-century European furnishings and objets d'art, all housed in a landmarked building. It's hard to describe what Gigantic Brand (49) *(59 Franklin St., Broadway/Lafayette Sts., 212-226-7214, www.giganticbrand.com)* sells exactly, but it's definitely worth the trip. The store bills itself as a "multi-media outlet," which includes fashion, electronics, comics, gadgets, and "other fun stuff" created by a group of international designers and housed in a very hip space. For Italian food, A. L. Bazzini Co. (50) *(339 Greenwich St., Harrison/Jay Sts., 212-334-1280, www.bazzininuts. com)* is the place to go. Bazzini's used to be a nut warehouse, so it uses the slogan, "more than just nuts," which indeed it is. They recently opened a terrific restaurant and deli featuring a selection of carefully chosen food products such as salad dressings, pastas, and yes, nuts. You can order stuff to go as well. Issey Miyake (51) *(119 Hudson St., Franklin/N. Moore Sts., 212-226-0100, www.isseymiyake.com)* is a suitably amazing space (it's designed by architect Frank Gehry) for Miyake's amazing men's and women's clothes. This sculptural chic will set you back, though. At Shoofly (52) *(42 Hudson St., Duane/Thomas Sts., 212-406-3270, www.shooflynyc. com)*, with its lovely European (mostly) children's

clothes, you can indulge your parental fantasies about what your little darlings really should look like. Archipelago (53) *(38 Walker St., Broadway/Church St., 212-334-9460, www.archipelagoinc.com)* is a must for high-thread-count addicts; it offers an enormous selection of linens, bedsheets, napkins, and more.

WHERE TO STAY

For visitors, Tribeca is a playground rather than a place to stay, though if you've got the money, the ultra-sleek 203-room boutique hotel the **Tribeca Grand (54) ($$$)** *(2 Avenue of the Americas, White/Walker Sts., 212-519-6600, www.tribecagrand.com)* is not a bad place to rest your head. A bonus of staying here is that the concierge can often get you a table at some of the tougher local restaurants to crack. More modestly, there's the 105-room **Cosmopolitan Hotel (55) ($$)** *(95 West Broadway at Chambers St., 888-895-9400, www.cosmohotel.com)*, which costs about a third of the price of the Grand and lacks its luxury design, but is one of the city's genuine bargains.

CIVIC CENTER

④ ⑤ ⑥ *to Brooklyn Bridge-City Hall;*
Ⓡ Ⓦ *to City Hall;* Ⓙ Ⓜ Ⓩ *to Chambers St.*

◦ SNAPSHOT ◦

When this area was first built up, it marked the northern edge of the city. When City Hall was being built in 1803, the northern façade of the building was left unfinished because no one thought the city would expand farther north. As was true then, this is where the city government resides. There are a number of imposing, majestic public buildings here. The Woolworth Building was the tallest building in the world from 1913 to 1929, until an uptown rival rose higher.

PLACES TO SEE
Landmarks:
City Hall (56), from which the mayor runs this vast megalopolis, is a white renaissance creation dating from 1812, set amid lovely gardens with fountains *(Vesey to Chambers Sts., Broadway to Park Row)*. City Hall and the immediate area are closed to the public, but the southern parts of the gardens are open to all. Across from it is the **Municipal Building (57)** *(1 Centre St. opposite Chambers St.)*, with its magnificent colonnade. Upstairs is the public marriage office and chapel, which is both an amusing and genuinely touching place to visit. The most striking building by far is the classic **Woolworth Building (58)** *(233 Broadway, Park Place/Barclay St.)*—a

Gothic masterpiece rising 792 feet, and the tallest building in the world when it opened in 1913. The superb lobby, with its mosaic ceiling and figurines—including one of Woolworth counting his money—is open to the public.

PLACES TO EAT & DRINK
Where to Eat:
This isn't a great area in which to eat, catering as it does mostly to a busy brown-bag grabbing workforce during the day. Your best bet is to slip off north and east to Chinatown, or west to Tribeca. If you do want to stay in the area for a quick bite, try **Fulton Street (59)** or **Beekman Street (60)**, where you'll find a variety of small, family-run delicatessens amid the Starbucks and McDonald's.

WHERE TO SHOP
One word rules here: electronics. Over the years, the family-owned J&R Music and Computer World (61) *(15-23 Park Row, Ann/Beekman Sts., 800-221-8180, www.jr.com)* has expanded to cover virtually all the southern end of Park Row. Cameras, DVDs, computers, CDs—these guys have it all at cheap prices, and are renowned for their friendliness and expertise.

chapter 2

CHINATOWN
LITTLE ITALY & NOLITA
LOWER EAST SIDE
EAST VILLAGE

Places to See:

1. Eastern States Buddhist Temple
2. Bowery Savings Bank
3. The Forward Building
4. Columbus Park
5. Museum of the Chinese in the Americas
19. Saint Patrick's Old Cathedral
20. Umberto's Clam House
21. Police Building Apartments
22. Feast of San Gennaro
39. Lower East Side Tenement Museum
40. Eldridge Street Synagogue
41. Arlene's Grocery
42. Rothko
43. Tonic
44. The Living Room
45. ABC No Rio
46. Landmark's Sunshine Cinema
60. Nicholas and Elizabeth Stuyvesant Fish House
61. 151 Avenue B

62. New York City Marble Cemetery
63. Grace Church
64. Tompkins Square Park
65. Cooper Union
66. Joseph Papp Public Theater
67. La MaMa E.T.C.
68. St. Mark's-in-the-Bowery Church
69. Bowery Poetry Club
70. KGB
71. Nuyorican Poets Café
73. St. Mark's Place
75. First Street Playground

Places to Eat & Drink:

6. HSF
7. N.Y. Noodle Town
8. Dumpling House
9. XO Kitchen
10. New Indonesia and Malaysia Restaurant
11. Ping's
12. Canton
13. Double Happiness
14. Happy Ending

18. Cantina 194
23. Caffe Napoli
24. Café Gitane
25. Lombardi's
26. Da Nico
27. Bread
28. Café Colonial
29. Peasant
30. Public
31. Caffe Roma Pastry
32. Mulberry Street Bar
47. Katz's Delicatessen
48. Bereket
49. 71 Clinton Fresh Food
50. Chibitini
51. Max Fish
52. 'inoteca
53. The Slipper Room
72. Boca Chica
77. Veselka
78. Second Avenue Deli
79. Little India
80. Raga
81. Frank
82. Flor's Kitchen
83. Dok Suni's
84. Sobaya
85. Mermaid Inn
86. McSorley's Old Ale House
87. Zum Schneider
88. Lakeside Lounge
89. Angel's Share

Where to Shop:
15. Kam Man Food Products
16. Mott Street
17. Ten Ren Tea and
    Ginseng Co.
33. DiPalo's Fine Foods
34. Italian Food Center
35. Do Kham
36. Lunettes et Chocolat
37. Ina Nolita
38. Sigerson Morrison
54. Orchard Street
55. Russ & Daughters
56. Guss' Pickles
57. Yonah Schimmel's
74. Tribal Soundz
76. Dinosaur Hill
90. Russian and Turkish Baths
91. Astor Place Hair
92. St. Mark's Bookshop
93. Kiehl's
94. St. Mark's Sounds
95. Kim's Video

Where to Stay:
58. Hotel on Rivington
59. Off Soho Suites Hotel
96. East Village Bed & Coffee

CHINATOWN

6 to Canal St.; **N R Q W** to Canal St.;
B D to Grand St.; **J M Z** to Canal-Centre Sts.

● SNAPSHOT ●

With its winding alleyways, open air markets, street vendors, Chinese signs, and crowds haggling in Cantonese over seafood so fresh it's still swimming in the tank, Chinatown has an old-fashioned and exotic urban atmosphere that makes it one of the favorite destinations for New Yorkers and tourists alike. Over the years Chinatown's boundaries have spread, eating into nearby Little Italy so there's barely a rump of it left. This expansion continues today as endless waves of Asian immigrants continue to pour into what is the largest Asian community outside Asia. With its crowded streets and high-speed pace, the atmosphere is always electric in Chinatown.

PLACES TO SEE
Landmarks:

Check out the rows of gleaming golden Buddha statues at the **Eastern States Buddhist Temple (1)** *(64 Mott St., Canal/Bayard Sts., 212-966-6229)*, then walk over to the **Bowery Savings Bank (2)** *(130 Bowery, Broome/Grand Sts.)*, designed by the famous New York architecture firm, McKim, Mead & White, in 1893. Its marble Corinthian columns and soaring ceilings won it landmark status in 1966. **The Forward Building (3)** *(173-175 East Broadway, Rutgers/Jefferson Sts.)* is an intriguing symbol of the continuing growth and vitality of Chinatown. Once the headquarters of a famous Yiddish newspaper, it is now a Chinese church. In nice weather, the locals play *mah-jongg* (a Chinese game using up to 144 tiles and played with four people) and practice *tai chi* in **Columbus Park (4)** *(Baxter, Bayard, and Mulberry Sts.)*.

Arts & Entertainment:

With its amazing cultural diversity, New York hosts many different ethnic and cultural events, but few come close to the extravaganza of the **Chinese New Year**, celebrated every February during a two-week period (the date changes slightly each year) with firecrackers, a huge procession with dancing dragons that snakes in and out of various restaurants, and of course masses of delicious food. It's centered on Mott Street *(212-484-1222 for details)*, but includes a number of locations. The **Museum of the Chinese in the Americas (MoCA) (5)** *(70 Mulberry St. at Bayard St., 2nd floor, 212-619-4785, www.moca-nyc.org)* is a little-known cultural attraction, but one definitely worth visiting. Set discreetly inside an old school building, it offers not only excellent temporary exhibitions, but also a permanent collection of artifacts, letters, and remarkable photographs documenting the lives of Chinese immigrants to this country.

Kids:

The **Chinese New Year** *(212-484-1222, www.nycvisit. com)*, with its firecrackers and dragon costumes, is fun for older kids if you're here in February, though toddlers might be scared. If your kids are slightly older and have reasonably daring food tastes (a big if), **HSF (6) ($)** *(46 Bowery, Canal/Bayard Sts., 212-374-1319)* is child-friendly (as are most Chinatown restaurants if they're not too high-end), and offers great *dim sum*.

PLACES TO EAT & DRINK
Where to Eat:

Chinatown has great street food. Vendors selling freshly cooked noodles, pancakes, and other Asian specialties park their carts up and down Canal Street. Any vendor who has a long line of customers waiting is a good bet. The budget traveler can eat very well here, but remember to bring cash: many restaurants do not accept credit cards. Although you can never choose wrong simply by looking in the windows and deciding where the Chinese eat, some reliable standards are these: **N.Y. Noodle Town (7) ($)** *(28-1/2 Bowery at Bayard St., 212-349-0923, cash only)* for—what else?—scrumptious noodles at a very low price. The **Dumpling House (8) ($)** *(118 Eldridge St., Grand/Broome Sts., 212-625-8008, cash only)* is a little hole in the wall that serves delicious dumplings. **XO Kitchen (9) ($)** *(148 Hester St., Bowery/ Elizabeth St., 212-965-8645, cash only)* specializes in the cuisine of Hong Kong. Can't quite decide on one flavor? Try the **New Indonesia and Malaysia Restaurant (10) ($)** *(18 Doyers St. at Chatham Sq., 212-267-0088)*.

Indonesian food is a little bit like Thai, a little bit like Chinese, a little bit like Indian, and it's very good. Fresh seafood and a slightly more upscale atmosphere are the draws of **Ping's (11) ($$)** *(22 Mott St., Mosco/Pell Sts., 212-602-9988)*—a Chinatown favorite. **Canton (12) ($$$)** *(45 Division St., Bowery/Market St., 212-226-4441)* is a 50-year-old family restaurant whose specialty is gourmet Cantonese.

Bars and Nightlife:
Double Happiness (13) *(173 Mott St., Broome/Grand Sts., 212-941-1282)* is a dark and intimate bar where you can sip a green tea martini and watch the hipsters at play, and **Happy Ending (14)** *(302 Broome St., Forsyth/Eldridge Sts., 212-334-9676)* offers cozy booths and, for the literati, the weekly Happy Endings Reading Series on Wednesday nights.

WHERE TO SHOP
Chinatown is a popular destination for bargain hunters. **Canal Street**, especially, is lined with shops selling cheap knockoff designer watches and gold jewelry. Stop in at Kam Man Food Products (15) *(200 Canal St. at Mulberry St., 212-571-0330, www.kammanfood.com)* for everything from dried jellyfish to cookware. Mott Street (16) is a good place to pick up cheap souvenirs like Chinese children's pajamas, beaded slippers, and bits of jade. If you're interested in alternative medicine, stop in at the Ten Ren Tea and Ginseng Co. (17) *(75 Mott St., Canal/Bayard Sts., 212-349-2180, www.tenrenusa.com)* and check out the jars of herbs and roots.

LITTLE ITALY & NOLITA

B D F V to Broadway-Lafayette;
N R W to Prince St.; 6 to Spring St.

◉ SNAPSHOT ◉

Since most of the immigrants (and their descendants) who once lived on or around Mulberry Street have moved out to other Italian neighborhoods or the 'burbs, the enclave of Little Italy is just a shadow of its former self. The crowds still come, however, to enjoy the restaurants, cafes, groceries, and the week-long Feast of San Gennaro every September. Nolita (North of Little Italy) is a new neighborhood, home to one-of-a-kind boutiques for the young and fashionable.

PLACES TO SEE
Landmarks:

Probably the most beautiful spot in the neighborhood is **Saint Patrick's Old Cathedral (19)** *(263 Mulberry St., Houston/Prince Sts., 212-226-8075, www.oldsaint patricks.com)*. Built 1809-1815 in a Gothic Revival style, it's the oldest Catholic Church in the city. **Umberto's Clam House (20)** *(178 Mulberry St. at Broome St., 212-431-7545, www.umbertosclamhouse.com)*, a very different historic landmark, is where Joey Gallo, a famous Mafioso, was shot to death in 1972. The **Police Building Apartments (21)** *(240 Centre St., Grand/Broome Sts.)*, built in 1905-1909, is a handsome Edwardian structure with a huge dome. The police department

37

vacated it in 1973, and 10 years later it was converted into cooperative apartments.

Arts & Entertainment:

Little Italy's pleasures lie mostly in strolling around its old tenement-lined streets, absorbing its plentiful street life and, of course, sampling its gastronomic delights. But every September Little Italy is host to the **Feast of San Gennaro (22)** *(Mulberry St., Canal/Houston Sts., 212-768-9320, www.sangennaro.org)*, a huge tourist attraction with endless food vendors lining the streets, and a Ferris wheel and other sideshow pleasures imported. Many New Yorkers avoid it like the plague, considering its charms to have vanished long ago, but there's no denying that at night, with the streets all lit up, it can be a romantic sight.

Kids:

Italy is a famously child-indulging culture, and kids are welcome in most of Little Italy's restaurants, though it's quite an urban area and otherwise not of the greatest interest to most young ones. If you're here in September, the **Feast of San Gennaro (22)** *(see "Arts & Entertainment," above)* will probably hold their atten-

tion most. **Caffe Napoli (23)** *(191 Hester St. at Mulberry St., 212-226-8705)* lets you take your time demolishing your plate of pasta and offers children's portions as well.

PLACES TO EAT & DRINK
Where to Eat:

Café Gitane (24) ($) *(242 Mott St., Houston/Prince Sts., 212-334-9552)*, right across the street from St. Patrick's, is a good place to sit, sip mint tea, nibble reasonably priced Moroccan specialties, and gaze on

the church with its peaceful, tree-shaded cemetery. **Lombardi's (25) ($)** *(32 Spring St., Mott/Mulberry Sts., 212-941-7994)* offers great New York pizza pies (no slices) in a turn-of-the century restaurant. **Da Nico (26) ($)** *(164 Mulberry St., Broome/Grand Sts., 212-343-1212, www.danicorest.com)* is a tiny, homey restaurant in the heart of Little Italy, featuring crusty coal-oven baked pizza and pastas. **Bread (27) ($$)** *(20 Spring St., Elizabeth/ Mott Sts., 212-334-1015)* has youthful crowds who come here for tasty paninis and pastas. **Café Colonial (28) ($$)** *(276 Elizabeth St. at Houston St., 212-274-0044)* offers Brazilian dishes, salads, and sandwiches, and, in the summer months, outdoor seating. **Peasant (29) ($$$)** *(194 Elizabeth St., Prince/Spring Sts., 212-965-9511)* provides rustic Italian cuisine served in a dim, romantic interior. **Public (30) ($$$)** *(210 Elizabeth St., Prince/ Spring Sts., 212-343-7011)* is great if you're tired of Italian, and want to join the trendy crowds enjoying Asian fusion cuisine.

Bars & Nightlife:

Have a cappuccino at the turn of the century **Caffe Roma Pastry (31)** *(385 Broome St., Mulberry/Mott Sts.,*

212-226-8413). If you want to feel like a star in your very own *Mean Streets*, **Mulberry Street Bar (32)** (formerly **Mare Chiaro**) (*176 Mulberry St., Broome/Grand Sts., 212-226-9345*)—an old dark dive complete with phone booth, photos of the owner posing with what was then a very downtown Madonna—will fit the bill. Order a cheap beer and play some Sinatra on the jukebox. For something more upscale and romantic, order a glass of fine Italian wine at the candlelit **Cantina 194 (18)** (*194 Elizabeth St., Prince/Spring Sts., 212-965-9511*).

WHERE TO SHOP

Go to DiPalo's Fine Foods (33) (*200 Grand St. at Mott St., 212-226-1033*) and the Italian Food Center (34) (*186 Grand St. at Mulberry St., 212-925-2954, www.ifc186. com*) for olive oil, fresh pasta, and made-on-the-spot hero sandwiches. Do Kham (35) (*51 Prince St., Mott/Mulberry Sts., 212-966-2404*), a Tibetan shop, has silk stoles, striking silver jewelry, and stunning fur-lined Tibetan hats. If, for some reason, you're in the mood for chocolates and a new set of glasses, why not pick them up together in the chicer-than-thou Lunettes et Chocolat (36) (*25 Prince St., Elizabeth/Mott Sts., 212-925-8800*). If you're a fashionista on a budget, Ina Nolita (37) (*21 Prince St., Elizabeth/Mott Sts., 212-334-9048, www.inanyc.com*) is a designer consign-

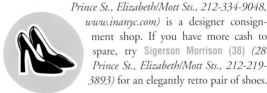

ment shop. If you have more cash to spare, try Sigerson Morrison (38) (*28 Prince St., Elizabeth/Mott Sts., 212-219-3893*) for an elegantly retro pair of shoes.

LOWER EAST SIDE

F to Delancey St.; *F* *V* to Second Ave.;
J *M* *Z* to Essex St.

◦ SNAPSHOT ◦

In the early years of the 20th century, the Lower East Side was the most densely populated area in the world. Primarily a Jewish neighborhood, its tenements were also crammed with immigrants from Eastern Europe, Italy, Germany, and Ireland, who worked in sweatshops and filled the streets with the  neighborhood's distinctive pushcarts. Although the living conditions, as revealed by the muckraking journalist, Jacob A. Riis, in his book *How the Other Half Lives*, were often grim, the denizens of the Lower East Side gave back much to America. George Gershwin, Ira Gershwin, The Marx Brothers, Al Smith, and many others were born or grew up here. In the 1960s, the ethnic makeup of the Lower East Side began to change as the older immigrant groups moved out and Hispanics began to move in. Drawn by cheap rents, many artists, musicians, and writers joined the mélange.

PLACES TO SEE
Landmarks:

For anyone interested in history, the **Lower East Side Tenement Museum (39)** *(108 Orchard Street, Broome/Delancey Sts., 212-431-0233, www.tenement. org)* is a must. The exhibits in this old tenement building recapture the daily life of the families that once lived here. The museum can only be seen by guided tour, so book ahead—the tours are very popular. Many of the area's synagogues have now been converted into other uses or are in extreme disrepair, but the **Eldridge Street Synagogue (40)** *(12-16 Eldridge St., Canal/ Division Sts., 212-219-0888, x205)*, the oldest, is still in use. Its elaborate Moorish interiors are currently being renovated.

Arts & Entertainment:

The Village Voice, *Time Out*, and *The New York Press* all provide listings for music around town. For live music, some good choices are **Arlene's Grocery (41)** *(95 Stanton St., Ludlow/Orchard Sts., 212-358-1633)* and **Rothko (42)** *(116 Suffolk St., Delancey/Rivington Sts., www.rothko nyc.com)*. For avant-garde and experimental music, there's **Tonic (43)** *(107 Norfolk St., Delancey/Rivington Sts., 212-358-7501, www.tonicnyc.com)*. The specialty of **The Living Room (44)** *(154 Ludlow St., Rivington/ Stanton Sts., 212-533-7235, www.livingroomny.com)* is singer-songwriters; it's where Norah Jones got her start. For poetry readings, **ABC No Rio (45)** *(156 Rivington St., Clinton/Suffolk Sts., 212-254-3697, www.abcnorio.org)* offers "Our Unorganicized Reading" open mike series every Sunday afternoon. And after all this, if you're in the mood for a movie, the **Landmark's Sunshine Cinema (46)** (*143 E. Houston St., First/Second Aves., 212-330-8182, www.landmarktheatres.com*), housed in what once was a Yiddish vaudeville theater, offers the kinds of independent art films you'd never find in your local multiplex.

Kids:

The Lower East Side is a dense urban neighborhood full of fascinating history and other adult attractions, but short on appeal for visiting children. However, if your children are somewhat adventurous eaters they'll probably love **Katz's Delicatessen (47) ($)** (*250 E. Houston St. at Ludlow St., 212-254-2246, www.katzdeli.com*), Yonah Schimmel's (57) (*137 E. Houston St., Forsyth/Eldridge Sts., 212-477-2858, www.knishery.com*), and Guss' Pickles (56) (*85-87 Orchard St., Broome/Grand Sts., 917-805-4702*) as much as adults do, and you can spend a few happy hours mutually cramming your faces in the name of "culture." For slightly older children, seven and up, the **Tenement Museum (39)** (*see "Landmarks," page 42*) may also prove of interest. The best playgrounds in the vicinity can be found in the East Village (*see East Village "Kids" section, page 51*), though you'll come across numerous **community gardens** as you stroll around the Lower East Side—most of which are usually pretty child-friendly.

PLACES TO EAT & DRINK
Where to Eat:

Katz's Delicatessen (47) ($) *(250 E. Houston St. at Ludlow St., 212-254-2246, www.katzdeli.com)*—grab a hot dog or a pastrami sandwich at this New York institution. **Bereket (48) ($)** *(187 E. Houston St. at Orchard St., 212-475-7700)* is a 24-hour joint to watch the hipsters devour inexpensive Turkish fast food. **71 Clinton Fresh Food (49) ($$$)** *(71 Clinton St., Rivington/Stanton Sts., 212-614-6960)* serves exactly that—exquisitely cooked new American cuisine in a pleasant, unpretentious setting.

Bars & Nightlife:

Chibitini (50) *(63 Clinton St., Stanton/Rivington Sts., 212-674-7300, www.chibitini.com)* is a cozy, crowded spot that specializes in sake. If you're there on the right night, you can grab some free dumplings, too. **Max Fish (51)** *(178 Ludlow St., Houston/Stanton Sts., 212-529-3959, www.maxfish.com)* has been going for longer than most of the trendsetters who pack it every night can remember. It's a curious place with a sense of décor that has to be seen to be believed, and has one of the most quintessential jukeboxes in the city, if you can hear it above the roar of the crowd. **'inoteca (52)** *(98 Rivington St. at Ludlow St., 212-614-0473, www.inotecanyc.com)* is a stylish place of brick walls and clean lines that serves an astounding number (more than 350) of wines by the

glass and bottle, with excellent bruschetta, cheeses, and other Italian delights. The staff is very knowledgeable, and even when the place is packed they'll take the time to answer your wine questions politely. **The Slipper Room (53)** *(167 Orchard St. at Stanton St., 212-253-7246, www.slipperroom.com)* is a long red room with booths on one side, a bar at the other, and a stage at the far end where patrons are treated to burlesque shows on weekends. It's quite expensive, but well worth the visit.

WHERE TO SHOP

Shopping in the Lower East Side is a rich cultural experience. The vendors on Orchard Street (54) may now speak Spanish instead of Yiddish, but they offer great bargains in clothing, shoes, and luggage. And if you're hungry, there's Russ & Daughters (55) *(179 East Houston St., Allen/Orchard Sts., 212-475-4880, www.russand daughters.com)* for lox and other smoked fish, Guss' Pickles (56) *(85-87 Orchard St., Broome/Grand Sts., 917-805-4702)* for pickles fished straight out of the barrel, and don't miss Yonah Schimmel's (57) *(137 E. Houston St., Forsyth/Eldridge Sts., 212-477-2858, www.knishery. com)* for a hot knish.

WHERE TO STAY

A hotel in the Lower East Side? A few years ago the idea would have seemed absurd. But it's a sign of the times that the spanking new **Hotel on Rivington (58) ($$$)** (*107 Rivington St., Essex/Ludlow Sts., 212-475-2600, www.hotelonrivington.com*) not only exists, but is also an ultra-ritzy glass-enveloped 20-story tower complete with every amenity you can think of. A beacon of cool. Also on Rivington, but a lot less splashy, is **Off Soho Suites Hotel (59) ($)** (*11 Rivington St., Bowery/Chrystie St., 212-979-9808, www.offsoho.com*), a strangely corporate name for what is a basic, good-value, no-nonsense place to stay.

EAST VILLAGE

6 *to Astor Place;* N R W *to 8th St.-NYU;*
B D F V *to Broadway-Lafayette St.*

◈ SNAPSHOT ◈

The East Village tends to blur, in many people's minds, with the Lower East Side—they're both grungy, hip, and full of old tenement buildings—and in a way it's true. But there are differences between the two neighborhoods, and for the purposes of this guide the East Village is considered to begin north of Houston Street, and the Lower East Side south of it. Both the East Village and the Lower East Side have taken on new, post-immigrant lives as hotbeds for the arts in the years since WWII. They became the places where artists, musicians, and writers congregated after Greenwich Village began its inexorable climb to bourgeois respectability and astronomical real estate prices. The Beat generation found succor here in the '50s and '60s; later, Punk Rock was nurtured at the infamous CBGB's club on the Bowery, and artists such as Keith Haring and Jeff Koons turned the East Village into the nation's hippest artistic center. Then in the '70s heroin hit the neighborhood badly. In the '80s real estate developers began to see promise in the area and the term "East Village" became a relatively new and distinct appellation for the neighborhood. The old

East Village did not go quietly into the night—there were riots in 1988 and 1995 as large numbers of squatters were evicted from its streets and parks, but its face inevitably began to change into what it is today, still an exciting, astonishingly multi-cultural human bazaar, but one with coffee shops (yes, Starbucks), delis, restaurants, and boutiques on every corner. Changed though it is, it remains one of the most vital parts of the city, and a stroll down its highly charged streets is mandatory for any pedestrian explorer of Manhattan.

PLACES TO SEE
Landmarks:

In the early 19th century the East Village was a wealthy middle-class neighborhood full of grand houses before the great waves of immigrants arrived in the late 19th century, followed in the 1950s by the raffish artists and other free spirits who turned it into New York's great Bohemia. Vestiges of this grand past can still be found amid the often-dreary tenement buildings, such as the **Nicholas and Elizabeth Stuyvesant Fish House (60)** *(21 Stuyvesant St., E. Ninth/E. 10th Sts.).* Built in the Federal style in 1803 for the great-grandson of the last Dutch general of what was then New Amsterdam, it's one of the earliest residential buildings in the city. Its generous proportions and handsome brick façade make a stark

contrast with the cramped dwellings that subsequent residents of the neighborhood usually endured. It's now owned by nearby Cooper Union and is the

official residence of its president. As well as tenement buildings, the East Village has a number of lovely brick and brownstone row houses dating from the mid-19th century. For a particularly fine example, check out **151 Avenue B (61)** *(E. Ninth/E. 10th Sts.)*, also known as "Bird's House," as its ground floor was home to saxophonist Charlie Parker from 1950 to 1954. The **New York City Marble Cemetery (62)** *(52-74 E. Second St., First/Second Aves., 212-228-6401, www.nycmc.org)* is another survivor of the neighborhood's solid past. Unless you gain entry on one of the occasional public tours, you can only get a tantalizing peek through the gate at this charming cemetery where some of New York's most illustrious citizens are buried, including the original inhabitant of the Stuyvesant Fish House. **Grace Church (63)** *(802 Broadway at E. 10th St., 212-254-2000, www.gracechurchnyc.org)* is one of the most beautiful churches in the city—a delicate Gothic Revival creation with a particularly lovely steeple, and surrounding gardens. It's open to the public and offers concerts. The East Village's main public space is **Tompkins Square Park (64)** *(E. Seventh to E. 10th Sts., Aves. A/B)*. Like so many other parks in the city, this one has seen a major and controversial overhaul in recent years that resulted in the eviction of a large number of homeless people and subsequent radical re-landscaping to avoid those hidden pockets where insalubrious elements might dwell. With the rampant gentrification of recent years it's now a safe and family-friendly environment, though this being the East Village, the cross-section of residents who hang out here is still pretty eyebrow-raising.

Arts & Entertainment:

Legend has it that there are denizens of the East Village who never go above 14th Street. Their feeling is: why bother? If they want history, they can always go to **Cooper Union (65)** *(30 Cooper Square, E. Eighth St./ Fourth Ave., 212-353-4100, www.cooper.edu)*, New York's first free nonsectarian college, where Abraham Lincoln gave his famous "Right makes might" speech. If they want drama, the **Joseph Papp Public Theater (66)** *(425 Lafayette St., Astor Place/E. 4th St., 212-539-8500, www.publictheater.org)* and **La MaMa E.T.C. (67)** *(74A E. Fourth St., Bowery/Second Ave., 212-475-7710, www. lamama.org)* offer edgier alternatives to Broadway. If literature is their love, the poetry readings at **St. Mark's-in-the-Bowery Church (68)** *(131 E. 10th St. at Second Ave., 212-674-0910)*, the **Bowery Poetry Club (69)** *(308 Bowery, Bleecker/Houston Sts., 212-614-0505, www. bowerypoetry.com)*, **KGB (70)** *(85 E. Fourth St., Second/ Third Aves., 212-505-3360, www.kgbbar.com)*, and the **Nuyorican Poets Café (71)** *(236 E. Third St., Aves. B/C, 212-505-8183, www.nuyorican.org)* beckon. But that barely scratches the surface of all the East Village has to offer. It has the liveliest street life and the best budget-restaurant scene in the city. And if one needs to recover from a night spent drinking too many mojitos at **Boca Chica (72)**, *(13 First Ave. at E. 1st St., 212-473-0108)*, or getting a tattoo in one of the parlors on **St. Mark's Place (73)**, **Tompkins Square Park (64)** *(E. Seventh to E. 10th Sts., Aves. A/B)* and the neighborhood's many community gardens are great places to sit in the shade and relax. Most of all, the East Village is the place where opposites mingle—New York's ultimate melting pot. In this neighborhood, it is easy to find Ukrainian, Hispanic, and Japanese émigrés, aging hippies, art students from NYU, slackers, hipsters, rock musicians, revolutionaries, and as the rents climb in this increasingly desirable neighborhood, even stockbrokers.

Kids:

The **First Street Playground (75)** *(Houston and E. First St., First/Second Aves.)* has plenty of shade and inventive climbing frames for younger children. **Tompkins Square Park (64)** *(E. Seventh to E. 10th Sts., Aves. A/B)* has no less than three separate and excellent playgrounds, complete with climbing frames, and all are safely enclosed from the street. There are also numerous highly funky and original children's stores around here. One of the best is Dinosaur Hill (76) *(306 E. Ninth St., First/Second Aves., 212-473-5850, www.dinosaurhill. com)*, which has a wonderful selection of wooden toys, puppets, wind-up toys, and other classics.

PLACES TO EAT & DRINK
Where to Eat:

Italian, Indian, Eastern European, Korean, Latin American, Mexican, even American—if you're looking for a great bargain meal, the East Village is the place to go. No matter what cuisine or ambience you're in the mood for, the East Village will probably have a restaurant to suit both your cravings and your pocket. On a cold winter's day, order a piping hot bowl of borscht at **Veselka (77)** *($) (144 Second Ave. at E. Ninth St.,*

212-228-9682), a gussied-up Ukrainian 24-hour-coffee shop (dig those crazy murals of East Village types on the walls), or a hot pastrami sandwich at the **Second Avenue Deli (78) ($$)** *(156 Second Ave. at E. 10th St., 212-677-0606, www.2ndavedeli.com)*. (Note the stars embedded in the sidewalk, honoring actors of the Yiddish theater.) East Sixth Street between Second and First avenues (and now extending a tad eastward to Ave. A) is known as **Little India (79)**. **Raga (80) ($)** *(433 E. Sixth St., First Ave./Ave A, 212-388-0957, www.raganyc.com)* is one of the tastier choices. Come early if you don't want to wait in line at **Frank (81) ($)** *(88 Second Ave., E. Fifth/E. Sixth Sts., 212-420-0202, www.frankrestaurant.com)*, a lively, homey restaurant that serves up heaping plates of Italian favorites. Ever have Venezuelan food? Go to **Flor's Kitchen (82) ($)** *(149 First Ave., E. Ninth/E. 10th Sts., 212-387-8949)* for inexpensive stews and empanadas served in a restaurant that is tiny, yet bright. Young hipsters love **Dok Suni's (83) ($$)** *(119 First Ave., E. Seventh St./St. Marks Place, 212-477-9506)* for its dark, dive bar décor and its garlicky Korean barbecue. If you have a yen for Japanese food, **Sobaya (84) ($$)** *(229 E. 9th St., Second/Third Aves., 212-533-6966)* serves up satisfying bowls of the noodles known as udon and a wide selection of Japanese beer. And if all this foreign food leaves you with a craving for Americana, get some fresh seafood at the **Mermaid Inn (85) ($$)** *(96 Second Ave., E. Fifth/E. Sixth Sts., 212-674-5870, www.themermaidnyc.com)*. Its wood-lined walls and casual décor evoke a New England fishing shack.

Bars & Nightlife:

The East Village has a hopping bar scene. Have a beer at the fabled **McSorley's Old Ale House (86)** *(15 E. Seventh St., Second/Third Aves., 212-473-9148)*. Opened in 1854, this little piece of old New York has sawdust on the floors, old newspaper clippings on the wall, and its own ale. **Zum Schneider (87)** *(107 Ave. C at E. Seventh St., 212-598-1098, www.zumschneider.com)* is a great place for German beer, with 12 kinds on tap. **Lakeside Lounge (88)** *(162 Ave. B, E. 10th/E. 11th Sts., 212-529-8463)* is where you can hear lively rock bands without paying either a minimum or a cover. And if you're in the mood for something more sophisticated, walk up the stairs of **8 Stuyvesant St.** *(St. Marks Place/E. Ninth St.)* and through the **Village Yokocho** Japanese restaurant into the tiny **Angel's Share (89)** *(212-777-5415)*. Collapse into one of the cozy armchairs and order a dry martini. Your Japanese waiter will mix it for you at your table. Enjoy it while gazing out the windows at Astor Place and the crowds below.

WHERE TO SHOP

The raffish **St. Mark's Place (73)** *(Eighth St., Third Ave./Ave A)* is a jumble of CD stores, head shops, comic book shops, T-shirt and cheap jewelry stands, cafes and bars, and is crowded day and night. East of First Avenue, **Avenues A** and **B** have an artier, edgier vibe. **East Seventh Street** and **Stuyvesant Street** (a one-block gem between St. Mark's Place on Third Avenue and East Ninth Street) are beautiful tree-shaded, brownstone-lined streets where many off-beat clothing and jewelry designers have set up shop. If it's all too much for you, take time for a shvitz (Yiddish for steam bath) at the Russian and Turkish Baths (90) *(268 E. 10th St., First Ave./Ave. A, 212-473-8806, www.russianturkishbaths.com)*. It's a perfect way to take a time-trip back to the days when the streets were packed with immigrants, Second Avenue was the Broadway of the Yiddish theater scene, and tenement apartments had a bathtub in the kitchen. If you're in the mood for something really different, pay the Russian masseuse to beat you with an oak branch—it's supposed to improve the circulation. Or join lines to get a cheap (and very memorable) haircut at Astor Place Hair (91) *(2 Astor Place at Broadway, 212-475-9854, www.astorplacehairstylist.com)*. Browsing (and even buying) is a major East Village sport. For books, try St. Mark's Bookshop (92) *(31 Third Ave., at E. Ninth St., 212-260-7853, www.stmarksbookshop.com)* for photography books, literary journals, and tons of trendy literati ambience. Kiehl's (93) *(109 Third Ave., E.13th/E.14th Sts., 212-677-3171, www.kiehls.com)*, a family-run pharmacy since the 19th century, now imports its distinctive lotions and shampoos, but the high-ceilinged emporium is still the place to go to be served by pleasant, knowledgeable salespeople in their pristine lab coats. St. Mark's Sounds (94) *(20 St. Mark's Place, Second/Third Aves., 212-677-3444)* is a great place for hard-to-find vintage vinyl, and Kim's Video (95) *(6 St. Mark's Place, Second/Third Aves., 212-505-0311)* has hard-to-find CDs. And if you're interested in making your own music, browse among the didgeridoos

(Australian Aboriginal musical instruments) at the one-of-a-kind music shop, Tribal Soundz (74) *(340 E. Sixth St., First/Second Aves., 212-673-5992, www.tribal soundz.com)*. St. Mark's Place between Second and Third avenues is the place for punk gear; First Avenue and Avenue A are good for vintage clothing.

WHERE TO STAY

The East Village Bed & Coffee (96) ($) *(110 Ave. C, E. Seventh/E. Eighth Sts., 212-533-4175, www.bedand coffee.com)* is one of the most unusual and certainly friendliest places to stay—a walk-up brownstone with chic rooms, a private garden for guests, plus live-in hostess and her dog. A real New York gem.

chapter 3

NOHO

SOHO

GREENWICH VILLAGE

UNION SQUARE

NoHo
SoHo
Greenwich Village
Union Square

Places to See:

1. Washington Square Park
2. Washington Mews
4. West Fourth Street
8. Electric Lady Sound Studios
9. Sullivan Street Playhouse
10. Jefferson Market Library
11. Patchin Place
12. The New School
13. Sheridan Square
14. 77 Bedford/75-1/2 Bedford
15. Church of St. Luke's in the Fields
16. Perry West
17. Meatpacking District
18. Cherry Lane Theatre
19. Actors Playhouse
20. Comedy Cellar
21. Bowlmor Lanes
22. Forbes Magazine Galleries
23. Grey Art Gallery
24. Carmine Street Playground
65. Union Square Greenmarket
66. 33 Union Square West
67. Union Square Theatre
68. Daryl Roth Theater
69. Vineyard Theatre
88. The Bayard-Condict Building
89. Bond Street Savings Bank
90. Fire Engine Company No. 33
91. DeVinne Press Building
92. Merchant's House Museum
93. Colonnade Row
95. Joseph Papp Public Theater/Joe's Pub
96. Amato Opera Theater
97. Bowery Poetry Club
98. Angelika Film Center
110. Singer Building
111. E. V. Haughwout & Co. Store
112. The Drawing Center
113. Artists Space
114. Deitch Projects
115. Phyllis Kind Gallery
116. Janet Borden Gallery
117. New York City Fire Museum

Places to Eat & Drink:

3. Cedar Tavern
5. Caffé Reggio
6. Café Borgia
7. Caffe Dante
26. Magnolia Bakery
27. Grey Dog's Coffee
28. John's of Bleecker Street Pizzeria
29. Corner Bistro
30. Florent
31. Moustache
32. Tea & Sympathy
33. Pastis
34. Babbo
35. Lupa
36. Jane
37. Chumley's
38. White Horse Tavern
39. Hogs and Heifers
40. APT
41. The Otheroom
42. Monster
43. Rubyfruit Bar & Grill
44. Village Vanguard
45. Blue Note
46. 55 Bar
47. Smalls
48. Zinc Bar
70. Chat 'n' Chew
71. City Bakery
73. Rainbow Falafel and Shawarma
74. Zen Palate

75. Union Square Café
76. Blue Water Grill
77. Republic
78. Old Town Bar & Grill
79. Pete's Tavern
80. Heartland Brewery
81. Underbar
82. Irving Plaza
99. Two Boots Restaurant
100. Noho Star
101. Great Jones Café
102. Five Points
103. Bond Street
104. Tom and Jerry's
105. Marion's Continental
106. B Bar
118. Hampton Chutney Company
119. Pepe Rosso To Go
120. Fanelli's
121. Jerry's
122. Balthazar
123. Blue Ribbon Sushi
124. Ear Inn
125. Broome Street Bar
126. The Room
127. MercBar
128. Bar 89
129. Performing Garage
130. Don Hill's
131. S.O.B.'s

Where to Shop:

Where to Stay:

NOHO

🅑🅓🅕🅥 *to Broadway-Lafayette St.;*
🌀 *to Bleecker St.*

⚜ SNAPSHOT ⚜

In the 1970s, this area of warehouses north of Houston Street (hence its acronym NoHo for "North of Houston Street") began to draw artists escaping from the escalating rents of neighboring Soho. In 1976, the neighborhood was rezoned so that artists could both live and work there. Today, Noho is a small, but bustling, neighborhood known as much for its popular restaurants and cabaret as for its arts scene.

PLACES TO SEE
Landmarks:

Dating from only 2000, the **Noho Historic District** *(roughly E. Houston St. to Astor Place, Broadway/Bowery)* is a fairly recent Landmarks designation, but it contains some astonishing buildings in a remarkable variety of styles and materials. **The Bayard-Condict Building (88)** *(65-69 Bleecker St., Broadway/Lafayette St.)* is an early skyscraper (13 stories!) and the only Louis Sullivan building in New York. Its lovely white terracotta façade was recently restored. The **Bond Street Savings Bank (89)** *(330 Bowery, Bond/Great Jones Sts., now the Bouwerie Lane Theater)* is a handsome cast iron building in a robust French Baroque style that's now home to the Jean Cocteau Repertory Company. One of the finest of all

New York's fire stations is the Beaux Arts **Fire Engine Company No. 33 (90)** *(44 Great Jones St., Lafayette St./Bowery)*. And in a different style altogether, go see the vast Romanesque bulk of the **DeVinne Press Building (91)** *(393-399 Lafayette St. at E. Fourth St.)*, which houses several fashionable antique stores and a restaurant on its lower level.

Arts & Entertainment:

The **Merchant's House Museum (92)** *(29 E. Fourth St., Lafayette St./Bowery, 212-777-1089, www.merchants house.com)* is like a little trip back to the 19th century. This delightful Federal house is decorated with the original furniture of the wealthy family that lived there for several generations, and offers exhibitions and tours that reveal early 19th-century domestic life. Another remnant of the elegant lives of this period's successful citizens can be found in the four remaining town houses of what was once called **Colonnade Row (93)** *(428-434 Lafayette St., Astor Place/Great Jones St.)*. Check out the plays at the **Joseph Papp Public Theater (95)** *(425 Lafayette St., Astor Place/E. Fourth St., 212-539-8500, www.publictheater.org)*. If you think going to the opera is an intimidating—and expensive—experience, the **Amato Opera Theater (96)** *(319 Bowery, E. Second/Bleecker Sts., 212-228-8200, www.amato.org)* is a family-owned, very intimate opera house. For poetry readings try the **Bowery Poetry Club (97)** *(308 Bowery,*

Bleecker/Houston Sts., 212-614-0505, www.bowerypoetry. com). The **Angelika Film Center (98)** *(18 W. Houston St. at Mercer St., 212-995-2000, www.angelikafilmcenter. com)* shows independent and art films. Come early to enjoy refreshments beneath a huge chandelier at the theater cafe.

Kids:

Maybe you think kids and opera don't go together, but the **Amato Opera Theater (96)** *(see page 61)* will prove you wrong. Once a month this family-owned theater puts on shorter versions of famous operas for kids and families: both cheap and fun.

PLACES TO EAT & DRINK
Where to Eat:

For great pizza at a great price, **Two Boots Restaurant (99) ($)** *(74 Bleecker St. at Broadway, 212-777-1033)* is both kid and adult friendly. The **Noho Star (100) ($$)** *(330 Lafayette St. at Bleecker St., 212-925-0070, www.noho star.com)* dishes up good burgers and other American food, and the lively **Great Jones Café (101) ($$)** *(54 Great Jones St., Bowery/Lafayette Sts., 212-674-9304)* has tasty Cajun cuisine. For a glimpse of more fashionable people at play, **Five Points (102) ($$$)** *(31 Great Jones St.,*

 *Bowery/Lafayette St., 212-253-5700)* features creative American cuisine, and **Bond Street (103) ($$$)** *(6 Bond St., Broadway/ Lafayette St., 212-777-2500)* is known for its sushi.

Bars & Nightlife:

Bar 288, also known as **Tom and Jerry's (104)** *(288 Elizabeth St., Bleecker/Houston Sts., 212-260-5045)*, has a wide selection of beers. **Marion's Continental (105)** *(354 Bowery, E. Fourth/Great Jones Sts., 212-475-7621, www. marionsnyc.com)* is a good place for martinis and retro-charm. And if you're in the mood to see and be seen go to the former gas station now known as **B Bar (106)** *(40 E. Fourth St., Bowery/Lafayette St., 212-475-2220)*. **Joe's Pub (95)** *(425 Lafayette St., Astor Place/E. Fourth St., 212-539-8770, www.joespub.com)*, located in the Joseph Papp Public Theater, is one of the most innovative and popular places to go for cabaret in the city.

WHERE TO SHOP

Along with art supplies, The Art Store (107) *(1-5 Bond St., Broadway/Lafayette St., 212-533-2444)* sells journals, stationery, and art books. If you're in the market for unique souvenirs, Bond No. 9 Fragrances (108) *(9 Bond St., Broadway/Lafayette St., 212-228-1732, www.bondno9fragrances.com)* sells elegant perfumes named after different New York City neighborhoods. For CDs, DVDs, and videos, Tower Records (109) *(692 Broadway, W. Third/W. Fourth Sts., 212-505-1500, www.towerrecords.com)* has an okay rock selection and an excellent classical and jazz section.

SoHo

Ⓝ Ⓡ Ⓦ *to Prince St.;* ⒸⒺ *to Spring St.;*
❻ *to Spring St.;* ⒷⒹⒻⓋ *to Broadway-Lafayette St.*

◉ SNAPSHOT ◉

The neighborhood now known as Soho has gone through many lives. In the years after the Civil War, its distinctive cast-iron warehouses housed many textile companies and other light manufacturers. By the mid-20th century, however, many of the manufacturers had moved on. Drawn by Soho's cobblestone streets, cheap rents, and huge loft spaces, many artists then made the neighborhood their own. In 1972, Soho was rezoned as a residential neighborhood as well as a manufacturing one, and the next year it was designated the SoHo Cast-Iron Historic District. Rents began to soar. Today, it is the rare artist who can afford a Soho loft. The once half-empty streets of Soho are now packed with locals and tourists who come for the upscale trendy shopping and the galleries and museums.

PLACES TO SEE
Landmarks:

In the 19th century, cast iron was a popular building material. Strong and easily molded, a cast-iron façade could add elegance and durability to a plain brick building. Soho has the largest collection of cast-iron buildings in the world. Both solid-looking and fanciful, these early precursors to the skyscraper give Soho a cinematic ambience. Some of the more famous buildings are the **Singer Building (110)** *(561-563 Broadway, Prince/Spring Sts.)* and the **E. V. Haughwout & Co. Store (111)** *(488-492 Broadway, Spring/Broome Sts.)*.

Arts & Entertainment:

The Drawing Center (112) *(35 Wooster St., Broome/Grand Sts., 212-219-2166, www.drawingcenter. org)* is a nonprofit gallery dedicated to promoting the art and appreciation of drawing. **Artists Space (113)** *(38 Greene St., Broome/Grand Sts., 3rd fl., 212-226-3970, www.artists space.org)* is another non-profit gallery that gives group shows focused on a theme. Many artists have gotten their start here. Among private galleries, **Deitch Projects (114)** *(76 Grand St., Wooster/Greene Sts., 212-343-7300, www.deitch.com)*, **Phyllis Kind Gallery (115)** *(136 Greene St., Houston/Prince Sts., 212-925-1200, www.phyllis kindgallery.com)*, and **Janet Borden Gallery (116)** *(560 Broadway, Prince/Spring Sts., 212-431-0166, www.janet bordeninc.com)* are some of the most interesting.

Kids:

The **New York City Fire Museum (117)** *(278 Spring St., Hudson/Varick Sts., 212-691-1303, www.nycfiremuseum. org)* is a 1904 firehouse that has a collection of old fire engines and equipment as well as displays dedicated to the history of firefighting, including the sad, heroic time during and after September 11, 2001.

PLACES TO EAT & DRINK
Where to Eat:

Hampton Chutney Company (118) ($) *(68 Prince St., Crosby/Lafayette Sts., 212-226-9996, www.hampton chutney.com)* offers snack foods from the subcontinent that make an inexpensive and tasty lunch. **Pepe Rosso To Go (119) ($)** *(149 Sullivan St., W. Houston/Prince Sts., 212-677-4555)* started as an Italian takeout joint, but has added a few tables. Good pasta, great prices. When Soho was still a nameless artists' and factory neighborhood, **Fanelli's (120) ($$)** *(94 Prince St. at Mercer St., 212-226-9412)*, a 19th-century bar, was practically the only watering hole. It still has a raffish, artistic air. Come for a beer, the good bar food, and a glimpse of what things used to be like not so long ago. **Jerry's (121) ($$)** *(101 Prince St., Greene/Mercer Sts., 212-966-9464, www.jerrysnyc.com)* has good American food and lively, celebrity-studded crowds. It's very popular, especially for brunch. **Balthazar (122) ($$$)** *(80 Spring St., Broadway/Crosby St., 212-965-1785, www.balthazarny. com)* is famous for its delicious French bistro food, turn-of-the-century French décor, and glamorous patrons. **Blue Ribbon Sushi (123) ($$)** *(119 Sullivan St., Prince/ Spring Sts., 212-343-0404, www.blueribbonrestaurants.*

com) is always crowded, though patrons say it's worth the wait. A favorite of chefs, who will stop by to have a bite after work.

Bars & Nightlife:

What would be an artists' neighborhood without an old, dark, dive bar or two? Soho has a fair number. Besides Fanelli's *(see page 66)*, there's the **Ear Inn (124)** *(326 Spring St., Greenwich/Washington Sts., 212-226-9060)*, which claims to be New York City's oldest bar, and the **Broome Street Bar (125)** *(363 West Broadway at Broome St., 212-925-2086, www.broomestreetbar.citysearch.com)*. For a quiet, more upscale evening, locals like **The Room (126)** *(144 Sullivan St., Houston/Prince Sts., 212-477-2102)* for a good selection of wines and beers in an intimate atmosphere. If you want to pretend you're a rock star, **MercBar (127)** *(151 Mercer St., Houston/Prince Sts., 212-966-2727, www.mercbar.com)* in the very hip Mercer Hotel, or **Bar 89 (128)** *(89 Mercer St., Broome/Spring Sts., 212-274-0989)* will provide the perfect settings. Spalding Gray got his start at the **Performing Garage (129)** *(33 Wooster St., Broome/Grand Sts., 212-966-3651)*. This alternative theater continues to be the home for a variety of innovative work. If you downed too many beers at the **Ear Inn (124)**, shake it all off to soul and hip hop at **Don Hill's (130)** *(511 Greenwich St. at Spring St., 212-219-2850, www.donhills.com)*, or dance the mambo or the merengue—or fake it—at **S.O.B.'s (131)** (Sounds of Brazil) *(204 Varick St., W. Houston/King Sts., 212-243-4940, www.sobs.com)*. This venerable club features live music not only from Brazil, but from all over Latin America, the Mideast, Africa, and the Caribbean.

WHERE TO SHOP

If you're in the market for ultra-chic, artsy clothing, and money is burning a hole in your pocket, Soho is the place. Anna Sui (132) *(113 Greene St., Prince/Spring Sts., 212-941-8406, www.annasui.com)*, Helmut Lang (133) *(80 Greene St., Spring/Broome Sts., 212-334-1014, www.helmutlang.com)*, Anthropologie (134) *(375 West Broadway, Spring/Broome Sts., 212-343-7070, www.anthropologie.com)*, and Prada (135) *(575 Broadway at Prince St., 212-334-8888, www.prada.com)* are just a few destinations. Add cooler-than-thou European shoes from Camper (136) *(125 Prince St. at Wooster St., 212-358-1842)* and Otto Tootsie Plohound (137) *(413 West Broadway, Prince/Spring Sts., 212-925-8931)*. To polish your look, go for cosmetics from the Swedish company FACE Stockholm (138) *(110 Prince St. at Greene St., 212-966-9110)*. Underneath it all, some sexy lingerie from Agent Provocateur (139) *(133 Mercer St., Prince/Spring Sts., 212-965-0229, www.agentprovocateur.com)* is a per-

fect choice. If you're on a tight budget, the Chinese department store Pearl River Mart (140) *(477 Broadway, Broome/Grand Sts., 212-431-4770, www.pearlriver.com)* sells gorgeous silk jackets, blouses, porcelain, teas, lighting, and souvenirs at bargain prices. And the collection of exquisite journals, stationery, and handmade papers at Kate's Paperie (141) *(561 Broadway, Prince/Spring Sts., 212-941-9816, www.katespaperie.com)* will make you want to write home.

WHERE TO STAY

The Larchmont Hotel (84) ($) *(27 W. 11th St., Fifth/Sixth Aves., 212-989-9333, www.larchmonthotel.com)* is great if you don't mind sharing a bathroom. This small hotel on a beautiful Greenwich Village street has tons of European-style charm: clean, nicely furnished rooms with ceiling fans, and continental breakfast. A tiny town house located in the West Village, the Abingdon Guest House (72) ($$) *(13 Eighth Ave., W. 12th/Jane Sts., 212-243-5384, www.abingdonguesthouse.com)*, is known for its handsomely furnished rooms and quiet, homey atmosphere, but be warned—it has no elevator. If you want to see how the very beautiful people live, The Mercer (86) ($$$) *(147 Mercer St. at Prince St., 212-966-6060, www.mercerhotel.com)* has high-fashion interiors, marble bathrooms, a 24-hour concierge and room service, in a heart-of-Soho locale. The Holiday Inn Downtown/ Soho (94) ($$-$$$) *(138 Lafayette St., Canal/Howard Sts., 212-966-8898, www.holidayinn-nyc.com)* is nothing fancy, but it's pleasant, clean, convenient, and much cheaper than the glitzy new hotels nearby.

GREENWICH VILLAGE

Ⓐ Ⓒ Ⓔ *to West Fourth St. or 14th St.;*
Ⓑ Ⓓ Ⓕ Ⓥ *to West Fourth St.;* **Ⓕ Ⓥ** *to 14th St.;*
❶ ❷ ❸ *to 14th St.;* **❶** *to Christopher St.*

● SNAPSHOT ●

"The Village," as it's known to New Yorkers, has long been a refuge. In the 17th and 18th centuries, it was a sleepy country town to which New Yorkers fled in order to escape various plagues. In the 19th century, Italian immigrants came, bringing their cafes, bakeries, churches, and pizzerias with them. These days, the crooked tree-lined streets of the Village have become prime celebrity-spotting territory, as many actors and models have made it their home. But more than anything, this neighborhood has always drawn those attracted by its air of tolerance. The list of writers, painters, actors, musicians, and revolutionaries who have lived or hung out in this neighborhood would fill an encyclopedia. Among them are Edgar Allan Poe, Mark Twain, Edna St. Vincent Millay, Richard Wright, Jack Kerouac, Edward Hopper, Cary Grant, John Barrymore, Bob Dylan, and

John Reed, and that's just for starters. The Village is also where many say the gay liberation movement was born—on June 28, 1969, to be exact, when a police raid on The Stonewall Inn, a gay bar at 51 Christopher Street, evolved into the Stonewall Riots. The Stonewall

Inn has moved to 53 Christopher Street, and the surrounding neighborhood, with its gay bars and clubs, is still considered a gay Mecca.

PLACES TO SEE
Landmarks:

There are two things to realize before you begin your tour of The Village. First, the Village was not built on a numbered grid system, the way most of Manhattan was, but grew organically out of a network of rural paths. The result is some crazy cartographical anomalies, such as the corner where West 12th Street crosses West Fourth. It's easy to get lost. But the Village is quite safe and very walkable, and as you turn down some surprising alleyway, you'll soon discover that getting lost is part of the fun. The other thing to keep in mind is that there are really two villages: Greenwich Village, whose central plaza is Washington Square Park, and the West Village, the area surrounding Sheridan Square.

A good place to start a Greenwich Village tour is at **Washington Square Park (1)**, at the base of Fifth Avenue. Once a potter's field and a site for public hangings, this park is a haven for guitar strummers, chess players, street performers, NYU students, and those reliving the area's beatnik past. Its most notable feature is the **Washington Square Arch** *(NE side of Washington Square)*, designed by the architect Stanford White and erected in 1895 to commemorate George Washington's inauguration. Check out the elegant

Greek revival town houses on **Washington Square North**. When they were built in the 1830s, they were some of the most exclusive residences in town. Henry James's grandmother owned one. Now most of them are owned by **NYU**. Its campus is scattered in buildings all over Greenwich Village. You might also want to peek in at **Washington Mews (2)** *(Washington Square North and East Eighth St.)*. This quaint cobblestone street was once where the horses of the aristocracy were stabled and the servants lived.

The streets around Washington Square were popular in the 1950s, 1960s, and early 1970s with abstract expressionists, folkies, beatniks, and war resisters. Artists Jackson Pollock and Mark Rothko liked to hang out at the **Cedar Tavern (3)** *(82 University Pl., E. 11th/E. 12th Sts., 212-929-9089)*. Washington Square South turns into **West Fourth Street (4)**, the inspiration for Bob Dylan's "Positively Fourth Street." Sullivan, Thompson, Bleecker, and MacDougal streets were once places to catch a wild poetry reading, buy some handmade sandals or silver jewelry, and sip a cappuccino in the days long before there was a Starbucks on every corner. The handmade sandals, and the beatniks who wore them, are

gone, but the old cafes remain, still pleasant places to while away an afternoon. Try **Caffé Reggio (5)** *(119 MacDougal St. at W. Third St., 212-475-9557)*, **Café Borgia (6)** *(185 Bleecker St., MacDougal/Sullivan Sts., 212-674-9589)*, or **Caffe Dante (7)** *(79 MacDougal*

St., Bleecker/W. Houston Sts., 212-982-5275). For those interested in the history of rock, there's Jimi Hendrix's **Electric Lady Sound Studios (8)** *(52 W. Eighth St., Fifth/Sixth Aves., 212-677-4700, www. electricladystudios.com).* The **Sullivan Street Playhouse (9)** *(181 Sullivan St., Bleecker/W. Houston Sts., 212-674-3838)* was the theater where the world's longest-running musical, *The Fantasticks*, enjoyed its 42-year existence. Its first cast, back in 1960, starred the late Jerry Orbach, of *Law & Order* fame.

Along with the Washington Arch, Greenwich Village's most distinctive architectural landmark is the **Jefferson Market Library (10)** *(425 Sixth Ave., W. 9th /W. 10th Sts., 212-243-4334).* This red brick castle with its fairy-tale watchtower was originally designed as a courthouse by the Central Park designer Calvert Vaux in 1876. Vacated in 1945, it stood empty for 20 years and was slated for demolition when the efforts of community organizers resulted in the current renovation. It was opened as a public library in 1967. There are some charming streets in this area. Among them are **Patchin Place (11)** *(off W. 10th St., Greenwich/Sixth Aves.),* a quiet iron-gated mews containing a number of three-story houses (4 Patchin Place was the home of poet e. e. cummings). **West 11th Street** *(Fifth/Sixth Aves.)* and **West 12th Street** *(Fifth/Sixth Aves.),* is where **The New School (12)** *(66 West 12th St., www.newschool.edu)*—founded by radical intellectuals in 1919—is located.

A walk west will take you toward Greenwich Village's other square, **Sheridan Square (13)** *(Commerce St./W. Fourth St./Seventh Ave.)*, though in true got-to-be-different Village style, it's actually more of a triangle. Nearby Bedford Street is known for two houses that stand next to each other: **77 Bedford (14)** *(Morton/Commerce Sts.)*—the Isaac-Hendricks House—the oldest house in the Village, built in 1799; and **75-1/2 Bedford (14)**, only 9-and-a-half-feet wide, once the home of Edna St. Vincent Millay and later John Barrymore. The **Church of St. Luke's in the Fields (15)** *(487 Hudson St., Grove/Christopher Sts., 212-924-0562, www.stlukeinthefields.org)*, built in 1822, is one of the lovelier churches in the city. And if you're getting tired of quaint, amble over to the glass towers of **Perry West (16)** *(176 Perry St., corner of West St.)*. This apartment complex, designed by the modernist architect Richard Meier and opened in 2003, has already become the home of such celebrities as Nicole Kidman and Calvin Klein.

Gentrification has transformed New York in the past 30 years. The **Meatpacking District (17)** is the latest neighborhood to have undergone the process. This four-block enclave of cobblestone streets near the waterfront was once the home of more than a dozen meat-processing plants. Some of the plants still remain, but they have to battle for space with bars, restaurants, and boutiques that sell exquisite little handbags and designer togs. The

Meatpacking District is best seen at night, when the combination of old warehouses, old memories, and up-to-the-minute bistros (with clientele to match) creates a very urban glamor.

Arts & Entertainment:

The famous poet and Greenwich Village resident Edna St. Vincent Millay was the founder of the **Cherry Lane Theatre (18)** *(38 Commerce St., Seventh Ave./Bedford St., 212-989-2020, www.cherrylanetheatre.com).* Begun in 1924, it was the first Off-Broadway theater, and still hosts experimental theater, mixing it with more main-stream productions. Its tiny space offers an intimate the-atrical experience. The **Actors Playhouse (19)** *(100 Seventh Ave. South, Bleecker/Christopher Sts., www.ny theatre.com)* is another famous Off-Broadway spot that garners widespread attention. If you like stand-up, the **Comedy Cellar (20)** *(117 MacDougal St., W. Third/ Bleecker Sts., 212-254-3480, www.comedycellar.com)* is one of the more prestigious places for comics, and big names such as Jerry Seinfeld and Ray Romano make fre-quent appearances to brush up on their audience skills. Like bowling, but kind of prefer drinking and flirting more? The gleamingly retro **Bowlmor Lanes (21)** *(110 University Place, 12th/13th Sts., 212-255-8188, www. bowlmor.com)* is for you, and you may well spot some of Hollywood's younger stars disporting themselves inappropriately. The Village, for all its attractions, isn't a museum hot spot, but it is the site of one of the

best, and certainly the quirkiest, small museums in New York, the **Forbes Magazine Galleries (22)** *(60 Fifth Ave. at W. 12th St., 212-206-5548, www.forbescollection.com, entrance is free)*. The late gazillionaire Malcolm Forbes was a man who liked to have fun, and the gallery is a memorial to his passions, from Fabergé Easter Eggs to toy boats and stray pieces of memorabilia, all arranged with wit and a touchingly personal sense. NYU offers its own exhibition space with the little-known but absolutely first-rate **Grey Art Gallery (23)** *(NYU Silver Center, 100 Washington Square East, corner of Washington Place, 212-998-6780, www.nyu.edu/greyart)*, featuring a 6,000-piece permanent collection of late 19th-century to early 20th-century art, including works by Picasso, de Kooning, and Miró.

Kids:

It may scare younger or more sensitive kids, but the annual **Halloween Day Parade** *(www.halloween-nyc.com)* that snakes its way up Sixth Avenue every October is incredible fun. A mix of ghosts, goblins, superheroes, stilt-walkers, drag queens, and, inevitably, endless Elvis Presleys, all wow the good-natured crowd. The **Carmine Street Playground (24)** *(32 Carmine St., Bleecker/Bedford Sts.)* is one of the best in the Village. Head through the narrow passageway into a delightful safe play area full of climbing frames and toys. Peanut Butter and Jane (25) *(617 Hudson St., W. 12th/Jane Sts., 212-620-7952)* offers cool clothes for kids, including a line of vintage items, as well as European toys and clothes.

PLACES TO EAT & DRINK
Where to Eat:

Although the Village certainly has some expensive (and worth it) restaurants, a budget traveler can eat extremely well here. In fact, some of the Village's most popular restaurants are also among its most reasonable. For breakfast, The **Magnolia Bakery (26) ($)** *(401 Bleecker St. at W. 11th St., 212-462-2572)* and **Grey Dog's Coffee (27) ($)** *(33 Carmine St., Bedford/Bleecker Sts., 212-462-0041)* are great places for coffee and baked goods. For New York pizza, **John's of Bleecker Street Pizzeria (28) ($)** *(278 Bleecker St., Sixth/Seventh Aves., 212-243-1680, www.johnsofbleeckerstreet.com)* has been serving customers brick oven pies since the 1920s. (The only caveat: John's does not serve slices, so bring a big appetite or a group to share a pie.) For great burgers, join the starving artists, students, and carnivores at the **Corner Bistro (29) ($)** *(331 W. Fourth St., Jane St./Eighth Ave., 212-242-9502, www.cornerbistro.citysearch.com)*. And after a night of clubbing, **Florent (30) ($$)** *(69 Gansevoort St., Greenwich/Washington Sts., 989-5779)* is a French bistro open 24 hours a day on weekends; come at four in the morning for a taste of the city that never sleeps. For inexpensive Middle Eastern fare, try **Moustache (31) ($$$)** *(90 Bedford St., Barrow/Grove Sts., 212-229-2220)*. On a rainy afternoon you might enjoy high tea at **Tea & Sympathy (32) ($$)** *(110 Greenwich Ave., W. 12th/W. 13th Sts., 212-989-9735, www.teaandsympathynewyork.com)*, served in an

eccentric English atmosphere. If you're in the mood for a blow out, try **Pastis (33) ($$$)** *(9 Ninth Ave. at Little 12th St., 212-929-4844, www.pastisny.com)* a raucous French bistro in the Meatpacking District, for oysters and a glimpse at the beautiful people. Italian food is always a good choice in the Village. Probably the most coveted table in town is at **Babbo (34) ($$$)** *(110 Waverly Place, MacDougal St./Sixth Ave., 212-777-0303, www.babbonyc.com)*, owned by superstar chef and local character, Mario Batali. Those on a more moderate budget might try another one of Batali's restaurants, **Lupa (35) ($$)** *(170 Thompson St., Bleecker/W. Houston St., 212-982-5089, www.lupa restaurant.com)*. Finally, if all this cosmopolitanism gives you a craving for good American food and moderate prices, **Jane (36) ($$)** *(100 W. Houston St., La Guardia Place/Thompson St., 212-254-7000, www.jane restaurant.com)* serves chops, seafood, and deliciously gooey desserts in an understated elegant setting.

Bars & Nightlife:

For a drink, **Chumley's (37)** *(86 Bedford St., Barrow/ Grove Sts., 212-675-4449)* is both a cozy watering hole and time capsule. A former speakeasy, it has no sign out front. Inside, the walls are decorated with photographs

and book covers of many of its famous patrons, including F. Scott Fitzgerald, John Steinbeck, and William Faulkner. In the winter, there's always a fire crackling in the grate. Another bar with literary connections is the **White**

Horse Tavern **(38)** *(567 Hudson St. at W. 11th St., 212-989-3956)*, where poet Dylan Thomas went on his last drinking binge before dying a few hours later. The former biker bar, **Hogs and Heifers (39)** *(859 Washington St. at W. 13th St., 212-929-0655, www.hogsandheifers.com)* is not nearly as down-and-dirty as it once was, though the girl bartenders still dance on the countertops, and the walls are decorated with discarded bras. For quieter evenings, try the glamorous lounge **APT (40)** *(419 W. 13th St., Ninth Ave./Washington St., 212-414-4245)* and the sophisticated **The Otheroom (41)** *(143 Perry St., Greenwich/Washington Sts., 212-645-9758)*. And if you're interested in the gay scene, the **Monster (42)** *(80 Grove St., Waverly Pl./W. Fourth St., 212-924-3558)* for men and **Rubyfruit Bar & Grill (43)** *(531 Hudson St., Charles/W. 10th Sts., 212-929-3343)* for women are old reliables. The Village is the home of some famous jazz clubs, such as the **Village Vanguard (44)** *(178 Seventh Ave. South, corner of W. 11th St., 212-255-4037)* and the **Blue Note (45)** *(131 W. Third St., MacDougal St./Sixth Ave., 212-475-8592, www.bluenotejazz.com)*. These famous clubs can be pricey, however. Some inexpensive (and very popular) clubs to try are the **55 Bar (46)** *(55 Christopher St., Sixth/Seventh Aves., 212-929-9883)* and **Smalls (47)** *(183 W. 10th St. at Seventh Ave., 212-929-7565)*. The **Zinc Bar (48)** *(90 W. Houston St. at La Guardia Pl., 212-477-8337, www.zincbar.com)* has Brazilian jazz and jazz vocals on Saturday and Sunday nights.

WHERE TO SHOP

One of the first fashion designers to head to the Meatpacking District was **Jeffrey New York (49)** *(449 W. 14th St., Ninth/ 10th Aves., 212-206-1272)*, whose simple yet stylish clothes attract models and actresses like moths to a flame. Somewhat more down-market is **Urban Outfitters (50)** *(374 Sixth Ave. at Waverly Pl., 212-677-9350, www.urbanoutfitters.com)*, which sells hipster gear for those on a budget. For something sexy to wear beneath, **La Petite Coquette (51)** *(51 University Pl., W. Ninth/W. 10th Sts., 212-473-2478, www.thelittleflirt.com)* is a good choice for gorgeous lingerie. New Yorkers looking for cheap fashionable shoes will browse the shoe stores on **East 8th Street (52)** *(Fifth/Sixth Aves)*. **C. O. Bigelow (53)** has been standing at 414 Sixth Avenue *(W. Eighth/W. Ninth Sts., 212-533-2700, www.bigelowchemists.com)* for more than 150 years. It offers a quirky collection of American and European lotions and soaps. The streets around Bleecker and Sixth Avenue have many shops catering to the music lover. For rare records try **Bleecker Bob's Golden Oldies Record Shop (54)** *(118 W. Third St., MacDougal St./Sixth Ave., 212-475-9677)* or **Bleecker Street Records (55)** *(239 Bleecker St., Carmine/Leroy Sts., 212-255-7899)*. **Matt Umanov Guitars (56)** *(273 Bleecker St., Sixth/Seventh Aves., 212-675-2157, www.umanov guitars.com)* has long been famous for its collection of both acoustic and electric instruments. One of the city's best independent bookstores is **Three Lives & Company**

(57) *(154 W. 10th St. at Waverly Pl., 212-741-2069, www.threelives.com)*, which has a knowledgeable staff and an excellent selection of literary fiction, biography, and memoirs. Shopping for food in the Village is an experience that is miles away from pushing your cart through the supermarket. Foodies swear by the venerable Murray's Cheese Shop (58) *(254 Bleecker St., Sixth/Seventh Aves., 212-243-3289, www.murrays cheese.com)*, opened in 1940. For a pound or two of freshly roasted coffee, go to Porto Rico (59) *(201 Bleecker St., Sixth Ave./MacDougal St., 212-477-5421, www.portorico.com)*, a family-owned business that began in 1907. For those who wish to satisfy other appetites, Condomania (60) *(351 Bleecker St. at W. 10th St., 212-691-9442, www.condomania.com)* sells a wider array of colored and flavored condoms than you can imagine, and the Pink Pussycat Boutique (61) *(167 W. Fourth St., Sixth/Seventh Aves.,*

212-243-0077, www.pinkpussycat.com) sells sex toys. And for a different kind of game, the Village Chess Shop (62) *(230 Thompson St., W. Third/Bleecker Sts., 212-475-9580, www.chess-shop.com)* sells chess sets and gives lessons. For the book lover, the world's largest used bookstore, The Strand Bookstore (83) *(828 Broadway, corner of E. 12th St., 212-473-1452, www.strandbooks.com)* is essential browsing. Its motto, before its recent expansion, was "eight miles of books." Now it's "eighteen miles of books."

WHERE TO STAY

It's expensive, but the Hotel Gansevoort (63) ($$$) *(18 Ninth Ave. at W. 13th St., 212-206-6700, www.hotel gansevoort.com)* in the Meatpacking District is a stylish new building with generous-sized rooms, a private roof garden, and a pool. The Washington Square Hotel (64) ($) *(103 Waverly Place, MacDougal St./Sixth Ave., 212-777-9515, www.wshotel.com)* is a comfortable 100-year old building in a great location across from the square. Rooms aren't big, but it's inexpensive and friendly.

UNION SQUARE

🄻 🄽 🅀 🄲 🅆 ❹ ❺ ❻ *to 14th St.-Union Square*

◦ SNAPSHOT ◦

Union Square is the city's most historic gathering place. It has been the scene of innumerable labor rallies and war protests and, in the days after September 11, 2001, it was also the site of a moving impromptu shrine. Though there are still protesters, most people come to Union Square these days either to sell vegetables or to buy them; the city's busiest farmer's market is based here. Union Square is also the center of a thriving restaurant-and-hip-hotel scene.

PLACES TO SEE
Landmarks:

On Tuesdays, Thursdays, and Sundays, Union Square is a busy transportation hub, a place to walk the dog and gape at the statues of George Washington, Lafayette, and Gandhi. On Mondays, Wednesdays, Fridays, and Saturdays, the farmers from the surrounding countryside move in. Even if you're not up for food shopping, the **Union Square Greenmarket (65)** *(N. end, Broadway/ Park Ave. S.)* is a good place to spot celebrity chefs, and celebrities shopping for flowers or fruit. In the 1960s, **33 Union Square West (66)** *(near corner of E. 16th St.)* was the home of something far less bucolic:

Andy Warhol's Factory. Those interested in New York history might want to take a look at the **Union Square Theatre (67)** *(100 E. 17th St., at Union Square East, www.nytheatre.com)*. In the 19th century, it was the headquarters of the infamous Tammany Hall, the corrupt political machine that robbed the city coffers, but gave back both Central Park and the Brooklyn Bridge, so perhaps it was a fair exchange.

Arts & Entertainment:

The major draw for most people here is the incredible **Greenmarket (65)** *(see "Landmarks," page 83)*, but if you're a theater fan, you're in luck: the area has two of the hippest and most fun theaters, the **Union Square Theatre (67)** *(100 E. 17th St., Park Ave. S./Irving Place, 212-307-4100, www.nytheatre.com)* and the **Daryl Roth Theatre (68)** *(20 Union Square at E. 15th St., 212-375-1110, www. darylroththeatre.com)* Both seem to specialize in putting on experimental and "out-of-the-box" shows (the infamous *De La Guarda*, which ran at the Daryl Roth, for example), full of messy audience participation that kids and teenagers love, though they may well leave theatergoers with more traditional tastes cold. The **Vineyard Theatre (69)** *(108 E. 15th St., Union Square East/Irving Place, 212-353-0303, www.vineyardtheatre.org)* also offers adventurous choices; *Avenue Q*, the Tony Award-winning musical, got its start here.

Kids:

Union Square has two playgrounds, enclosed and with safety rubber matting, though they can get pretty crowded. Older kids will enjoy the skateboarding opportunities afforded by the northern end of the square when the Greenmarket is not in operation, which is safely cordoned off from traffic.

PLACES TO EAT & DRINK
Where to Eat:

Eating in this area can be expensive. But good, reasonable, All-American comfort food can be found at **Chat 'n' Chew (70) ($)** *(10 E. 16th Street, Fifth Ave./Union Square West, 212-243-1616)*. **City Bakery (71) ($$)** *(3 W. 18th St., Fifth/Sixth Aves., 212-366-1414, www.thecity bakery.com)* serves salads, sandwiches, and soups as well as coffee and baked goods. For great Middle Eastern sandwiches, **Rainbow Falafel and Shawarma (73) ($$)** *(26 E. 17th St., Fifth Ave./Broadway, 212-691-8641, takeout only)* is the place. For vegetarian food, try **Zen Palate (74) ($$)** *(34 Union Square East at E. 16th St., 212-614-9291, www.zenpalate.com)*. If you can afford it, Union Square is known for its chic restaurants. The one that started it all is the **Union Square Café (75) ($$$)** *(21 E. 16th St., Fifth Ave./Union Square West, 212-243-4020)*. Its friendly service and creative American cuisine make it one of the most popular restaurants in New York. Some other good choices are the **Blue Water Grill (76) ($$$)** *(31 Union Square West. at E. 16th St., 212-675-9500, www.brguestrestaurants.com)* for seafood, and **Republic (77) ($)** *(37 Union Square West, 16th/17th Sts., 212-627-7172, www.thinknoodles.com)* for innovative Pan-Asian noodle dishes.

Bars & Nightlife:

If you're a fan of late night talk shows, the **Old Town Bar & Grill (78)** *(45 E. 18th St., Broadway/Park Ave. South, 212-529-6732, www.oldtownbar.com)* might look familiar: it's featured in the opening credits of *The Late Show with David Letterman*. This 19th-century tavern is a great place to grab a beer and good bar food. **Pete's Tavern (79)** *(129 E. 18th St. at Irving Pl., 212-473-7676, www.petestavern.com)* is another old bar: supposedly O. Henry hung out here. For women who love frat boys and the frat boys who love beer, **Heartland Brewery (80)** *(35 Union Square West, E. 16th/E. 17th Sts., 212-645-3400, www.heartlandbrewery.com)* might do the trick. And if you're looking for something exclusive and quietly hip, go to **Underbar (81)** *(201 Park Ave. South at E. 17th St., 212-358-1560)* inside the trendy W New York-Union Square Hotel (87). **Irving Plaza (82)** *(17 Irving Pl., E. 15th/16 Sts., 212-777-6800, www.irvingplaza.com)* is one of the best rock music clubs in town, host to medium-sized bands and the occasional big name playing a smaller show.

WHERE TO SHOP

Some of the great stores of New York are located in the streets around Union Square. For sporting goods, Paragon Sports (85) *(867 Broadway at E. 18th St., 212-255-8036, www.paragonsports.com)* is a local favorite.

WHERE TO STAY

If you don't mind forking out some serious dough, there's always the W New York-Union Square Hotel (87) ($$$) *(201 Park Ave. South at E. 17th St., 212-253-9119, www.starwoodspecialoffers.com/w_union_square/)*.   It's housed in a fabulous old building just off Union Square, and has a handsome bar on the ground floor in which to watch the elegant clientele at play.

chapter 4

CHELSEA

GARMENT DISTRICT

TIMES SQUARE-THEATER DISTRICT

& CLINTON

CHELSEA
GARMENT DISTRICT
TIMES SQUARE-
THEATER DISTRICT
& CLINTON

Places to See:

1. Chelsea Hotel
2. 437-459 West 24th Street
3. Cushman Row
4. Starrett-Lehigh Building
5. High Line
6. London Terrace
7. Chelsea Piers
8. Hudson River Park
9. Dia: Chelsea
10. The Kitchen
11. Museum at the Fashion Institute of Technology
12. Joyce Theater
13. Madison Square Garden
39. Lesbian, Gay, Bisexual & Transgender Community Center
40. Gay Men's Health Crisis
44. New York Times Building (original)
45. New York Times Building (current)
46. NASDAQ Electronic Stock Market Building
47. Reuters Building
48. Condé Nast Building
49. Penn Station
50. Brill Building
51. Music Row
52. Time & Life Building
53. Lyceum Theatre
54. Ed Sullivan Theater
56. Winter Garden Theater
57. Al Hirschfeld Theater
58. TKTS Booth
59. Times Square Visitors Center
60. Carnegie Hall/Zankel Hall
62. Town Hall
63. Madame Tussaud's New York
64. Circle Line
65. Intrepid Sea-Air-Space Museum
66. New Amsterdam Theatre
67. New Victory Theater
85. Macy's
86. Herald Square
87. Greeley Square
88. General Post Office

Places to Eat & Drink:

Where to Shop:

Where to Stay:

CHELSEA

A C E *to 14th Street;* **C E** *to 23rd Street;*
1 *to 18th St. or 23rd St.*

◈ SNAPSHOT ◈

Originally the country estate of a sea captain, Chelsea
evolved into a sophisticated urban area with handsome
Greek and Italian town houses, great swaths of which
still survive and make it one of the most desirable residential areas in the city. Nowadays, Chelsea is primarily
renowned for two things that other neighborhoods were
once famous for: the gay scene, which has largely
migrated from the Village; and the art scene, which
became increasingly priced out of Soho. There's also
Chelsea's waterfront, which in recent years has seen
remarkable development, as have long stretches of the
rest of the city's long-neglected waterfront.

PLACES TO SEE
Landmarks:

If it's your first visit to Chelsea, don't miss a visit to the
legendary **Chelsea Hotel (1)** *(222 West 23rd St.,
Seventh/Eighth Aves., 212-243-3700, www.hotelchelsea.
com).* This wonderful building with its beautiful rows
of cast-iron balconies started life as one of the city's
first co-ops, before becoming a hotel in 1905. Its
famous clientele has included Tennessee Williams,
Mark Twain, Bob Dylan, and Sid Vicious to name a
few—but it's far from a museum. It's still a privately

operated hotel, and its art-filled lobby and genuinely unconventional clientele offers a real glimpse of pre-Starbucks and chain-store NYC. Check out its basement bar, **Serena** *(212-255-4646, www.serenanyc.com)*, for cocktails and vaguely Eastern stylings. For architecture buffs, two blocks in particular are outstanding for their surviving period details: **437-459 West 24th Street (2)** *(Ninth/Tenth Aves.)*—a row of late Italianate brick houses—and the so-called **Cushman Row (3)** *(406-418 W. 20th St., Ninth/Tenth Aves.)*. On a more modern note, the **Starrett-Lehigh Building (4)** *(601-625 W. 26th St., Eleventh/Twelfth Aves., www.starrett-lehighbuilding.com)* is one of the city's gems. Designed as a warehouse in 1930-1931, complete with rail tracks leading directly into it, it now leads a less rugged life as home to a cluster of Web designers, media outlets, and the like. It's not a building, but one of Chelsea's most interesting landmarks is the **High Line (5)**, a long-defunct elevated rail track that runs above and just west of Tenth Avenue from around 12th Street to 30th Street, entering and exiting numerous industrial buildings. Plans are afoot to turn it into a park, though there is a considerable way to go before this idea becomes a reality. Confirming that everything New York is on a grand scale, **London Terrace (6)** *(W. 23rd-W. 24th Sts., Ninth/Tenth Aves., www. londonterracetowers.com)* is a vast apartment building with more than 4,000 rooms occupying an entire square block. Its original developer, who envisioned it as a bastion of British chic complete with doormen dressed as British Bobbies, went bankrupt in the 1930s, and threw himself off the roof. You may see professional dog-walkers and their noisy packs entering or exiting the building. Heading over to the river you'll encounter one of New York's most popular attractions, **Chelsea Piers (7)** *(Piers 59-62, W. 17th/W. 23rd Sts., Eleventh Avenue to the Hudson River, 212-336-6666, www.chelseapiers.com)*, which houses a vast sports complex where you can rock climb, bowl, in-line skate, roller-skate, shoot hoops, and even whack golf balls into a vast net over the Hudson River. There are also a number of bars and restaurants, and fancy docking facilities for the private yachts that berth here. Opinion is divided about all this: some see it as brash commercialism, others as an innovative use of what was once a decaying waterfront that previously offered no access to the public. If Chelsea Piers isn't your thing, you can simply walk or blade away along the waterfront esplanade and park that forms the **Hudson River Park (8)** *(www.hudsonriverpark.org)*, which under various guises forms a border of green along almost the entire west side of Manhattan.

GAY CHELSEA

There are numerous publications that list gay and lesbian events around the city, many of which are free and available in street corner boxes. In particular, check out weeklies *HX*, *Next*, *Gay City News*, and *New York Blade*. Gay and lesbian visitors can count on the **Lesbian, Gay, Bisexual & Transgender Community Center (39)** *(208 W. 13th St., Seventh/Eighth Aves., 212-620-7310, www.gaycenter.org)*, located slightly south of Chelsea on 13th Street, for information on anything from health issues to simply what's happening around town. More specifically for HIV counseling and advice, there's the venerable **Gay Men's Health Crisis (40)** *(119 W. 24th Street, Sixth/Seventh Aves., Ste. 6, 212-367-1000, www.gmhc.org)*. There are countless bars to suit every taste, but **Barracuda (41)** *(275 W. 22nd St., Seventh/Eighth Aves., 212-645-8613, cash only)*, is friendly if too vanilla for some tastes, and **Cafeteria (42)** *(119 Seventh Ave. at 17th St., 212-414-1717)* is a 24-hour gay-centric restaurant serving a variety of foods from healthy to heavy. If you're looking for a specifically gay place to stay, try the Chelsea Mews Guest House (43) *(344 W. 15th St., Eighth/Ninth Aves., 212-255-9174, cash only)*.

Arts & Entertainment:

Chelsea is the commercial art gallery center of New York, and your best bet to appreciate the almost overwhelming scene here is to simply wander up and down Chelsea's streets west of Ninth Avenue: you'll probably discover a show opening. But whatever you do, don't miss **Dia: Chelsea (9)** *(548 W. 22nd St., Tenth/Eleventh Aves., 212-989-5566, www.diachelsea.org)*, perhaps the most important gallery of them all. Established in 1987, Dia has become most well known for its concentration on exhibits by single artists, allowing them to stretch out and use the full space of the gallery. Richard Serra, Dan Flavin, and Bruce Nauman are among the big names that have exhibited here. **The Kitchen (10)** *(512 W. 19th St., Tenth/Eleventh Aves., 212-255-5793, www.the kitchen.org)* is another big Chelsea draw, offering a gallery and a constantly changing series of live performance and video art. The **Museum at the Fashion Institute of Technology (11)** *(Seventh Ave. at W. 27th St., 212-217-5970, www.fitnyc.edu)*, an exhibition space attached to this famous powerhouse of New York design, offers immaculately curated shows related to fashion and its social impact. Chelsea is more than just galleries, however, and if you love contemporary dance, the **Joyce Theater (12)** *(175 Eighth Ave. at W. 19th St., 212-242-0800, www.joyce.org)* is not only one of the most beautiful theaters, but also offers some of the most innovative programming, such as the Ballet Hispanico.

Kids:

If you're looking for something for that baby or toddler, visit Buy Buy Baby (14) *(270 Seventh Ave., W. 25th/W. 26th Sts., 917-344-1555)*, a Mecca for cool clothes like Carter's, stylish strollers, and more.

PLACES TO EAT & DRINK
Where to Eat:

For reasonably priced Italian, **La Bottega (15) ($$)** *(Maritime Hotel, 88 Ninth Ave. at W. 17th St., 212-243-8400)* is a good bet. With its pretty lanterns and plantings it's easy to forget its outside area is set in the plaza of a hideous 1960s monolith. If you're over by the **Starrett-Lehigh Building (4)** or checking out galleries, **Bottino (16) ($$$)** *(246 Tenth Ave., W. 24th/W. 25th Sts., 212-206-6766)* is a beautifully minimalist place to stop by for a drink or enjoy a Tuscan meal in one of its two dining rooms. **La Lunchonette (17) ($$$)** *(130 Tenth Ave. at W. 18th St., 212-675-0342)* offers delicious French bistro food in a long, low, and intimate setting. At **Salsa y Salsa (18) ($$)** *(206 Seventh Ave., W. 21st/W. 22nd Sts., 212-929-2678)* you'll find good Mexican standards and great drinks. For classic American fare, you can't beat the **Empire Diner (19) ($$)** *(210 Tenth Avenue at W. 22nd St., 212-243-2736)*, open 24 hours a day, and with a great outdoor seating area in warm weather. In a similar vein,

try **Better Burgers (20) ($)** *(178 Eighth Ave. at W. 19th St., 212-989-6688, www.betterburgernyc.com)* for calorie-specific (and antibiotic-free) burgers and fries—you can check out the calorie count of what you're eating on its Web site! For soup and salad lovers, the mini-chain **Hale and Hearty Soups (21) ($)** *(Chelsea Market, 75 Ninth Ave., W. 15th/W. 16th Sts., 212-255-2400)* offers tasty and healthy food to go. Finally, if you just want a sugar rush, there's no place better than **Krispy Kreme Doughnuts (22) ($)** *(265 W. 23rd St., Seventh/Eighth Aves., www.krispykreme.com)* for classic melt-in-your-mouth donuts.

Bars & Nightlife:

For drinks, **The Half King Bar (23)** *(505 W. 23rd St. at Tenth Ave., 212-462-4300, www.halfking.com)*, part-owned by author Sebastian Junger, offers perfect pub-grub and pints. **Peter McManus (24)** *(152 Seventh Ave. at W. 19th St., 212-929-9691)* is a classic no-frills Irish bar, and the **Trailer Park Lounge (25)** *(271 W. 23rd St., Seventh/Eighth Aves., 212-463-8000)* has some frills—if you consider white-trash kitsch a frill, that is. Away from most major residential areas, the far West Side is where many of the city's nightclubs are located. Venues change constantly, so it's best to get one of the many free local publications. **Lotus (26)** *(409 W. 14th St., Ninth/Tenth Aves., 212-243-4420, www.lotusnewyork.com)* is one of the more notorious. If you like velvet ropes and long lines, this is the place for you. On a more mellow note, nightlife staple **Lot 61 (27)** *(550 W. 21st St. at Eleventh Ave., 212-243-6555)*, owned by nightclub queen Amy Sacco, is a good choice for martinis and star-spotting.

WHERE TO SHOP

If you've got the right body (and wallet), Comme des Garçons (28) *(520 W. 22nd St., Tenth/Eleventh Aves., 212-604-9200)* has those minimalist pants and dresses you desire, and Beatle's daughter Stella McCartney (29) *(429 W. 14th St., Ninth Ave./Washington St., 212-255-1556, www.stellamccartney.com)* has her eponymous boutique here, too. For more affordable stuff, Loehmann's (30) *(101 Seventh Ave., W. 16th/W. 17th Sts., 212-352-0856, www.loehmanns.com)* offers designer clothes at discount prices. For housewares, Bodum (31) *(413-415 W. 14th St., Ninth/Tenth Aves., 212-367-9125, www.bodumusa.com)* has great kitchen items, and Details (32) *(142 Eighth Ave., W. 16th/W. 17th Sts., 212-366-9498)* will sort out your bathroom. If you're a jazz fan, the Jazz Record Center (33) *(236 W. 26th St., Seventh/Eighth Aves., 8th floor, 212-675-4480, www.jazz recordcenter.com)* is a real find. The Annex Antiques Fair & Flea Market (34) *(Sixth Ave., W. 24th/W. 27th Sts., 212-243-5343, cash only)* is a great place to ferret out a bargain, whether it's a piece of retro clothing or a deco coffee pot, though real bargain hunters get there early (as in sunrise). And if it's raining on the market, there's also an indoor location called The Garage (35) *(112 W. 25th St., Sixth/Seventh Aves., 212-647-0707).* Chelsea Market (36) *(75 Ninth Ave., W. 15th/W. 16th Sts., www.chelseamarket. com)* has a wonderful food court that sells everything from freshly baked breads to wine and flowers.

WHERE TO STAY

There's always the **Chelsea Hotel (1) ($$)** *(see "Landmarks," on page 91)* if you think you'll fit the scene, or check out the **Chelsea Lodge (37) ($$)** *(318 W. 20th St., Eighth/Ninth Aves., 212-243-4499, www. chelsealodge.com),* set in a discreet brownstone building, or the **Chelsea Star Hotel (38) ($)** *(300 W. 30th St. at Eighth Ave., 212-244-7827),* which offers funky rooms at middling prices, as well as can't-be-beat shared dorms for around $30 a night.

GARMENT DISTRICT

A C E *to 34th St.;* **1 2 3** *to 34th St.–Penn Station;*
B D F V **N Q R W** *to 34th St.*

❖ SNAPSHOT ❖

Slightly south of Times Square *(approximately W. 28th to W. 40th Sts./Sixth to Eighth Aves.)* lies the Garment District, containing New York's clothing industry. You'll know you're there when you stumble upon racks of clothes being wheeled across the street. Take a peep—you're looking at next season's high fashion. You'll also find button, fur, and fabric shops dotted around this neighborhood.

PLACES TO SEE
Landmarks:

The biggest of them all, of course, is **Macy's (85)** *(151 W. 34th St., Broadway/Seventh Ave., 212-695-4400, www.macys.com)*. From designer clothes to pepper grinders, this block-sized megalith's got it all, as well as a good restaurant for adults and a McDonald's for the kids. Right opposite is **Herald Square (86)** *(1328 Broadway at 34th St.)*, and at its southern end **Greeley Square (87)**, which has fairly recently been turned from a shabby no-man's land into an attractive space with tables and chairs in which to take a breather. If Macy's doesn't satisfy your shopping jones, try **H & M (55)** *(2 Herald Square, 212-564-9922,* *www.hm.com*). It's particularly good for kids' and teens' clothes. Another big landmark in the area is **Madison Square Garden (13)** *(Seventh Ave., W. 31st/W. 33rd Sts., 212-465-6741, www.thegarden.com)*. As New Yorkers love to point out, it isn't on Madison, it isn't a square, and it isn't a garden, but otherwise it lives up to its reputation as "the world's most famous arena," home to pro basketball and hockey games, circuses, concerts, and more. Be warned: basketball tickets for the New York Knicks are almost impossible to get, though you can try the box office on game day. Below the ugly (even New Yorkers admit it) hulk of MSG lies **Penn Station (49)**, an equally unlovely station, built in the '60s on the ashes of the fabulous old station, whose demolition sparked the landmark movement. Fortunately, plans are afoot to restore the magnificent McKim, Mead & White **General Post Office (88)** *(Eighth Ave., W. 31st/W. 33rd Sts.)* nearby, with its massive columned façade, into the new arrival terminal for Penn Station, which will also include links to JFK airport.

WHERE TO SHOP

The Garment District has some good, if not overly flashy shopping options. Victoria's Secret (61) *(1328 Broadway at 34th St., 212-356-8383, www.victoriassecret.com)*, that arch purveyor of sexy lingerie, has its flagship store right here in the Garment District, with a huge range of items available. It even offers personalized bra fittings, should you be so inclined.

TIMES SQUARE-THEATER DISTRICT & CLINTON

Ⓐ Ⓒ Ⓔ *to 42nd St.-Port Authority Bus Terminal;*
Ⓝ Ⓠ Ⓡ Ⓦ ❶❷❸ ❼ Ⓢ *to 42nd St.-Times Square*

◦ SNAPSHOT ◦

In classic New York style, the city's most famous square is not a square at all, but the arrowhead where two major thoroughfares—Broadway and Seventh Avenue—meet. In 1905 it acquired its modern name when The *New York Times* newspaper moved uptown to occupy the spot, marking the occasion with a massive New Year's Eve fireworks display that ushered in the role for which the site has become famous. The *New York Times* subsequently decamped to 43rd Street and the old building quickly became a peculiarly American icon as its owners realized it was worth more as a giant billboard than a functioning building. (Today, the area is so well associated with advertising that the Landmarks Commission, in a bizarre ruling, actually requires new buildings in the area to smother their facades with billboards.) With the *New York Times* as its commercial linchpin, theater houses flocked uptown, and by the early 1920s the area had become the city's principal theatrical neighborhood, followed a few years later by the movie theaters. The movie theaters have by and large all gone, but Times Square remains New York's theatrical center, with all the major theaters concentrated on or just off Broadway from the 40s through the 50s. More than 100 years from when the first theaters were built, it's still the place to come to see the latest drama, musical, or revue. Times Square is, of course, famous for its sleaze, and while pockets of XXX-related businesses still linger on (generally west of Eighth Avenue), the past ten years or so have seen a major face-lift and a return—hotly debated by some New Yorkers—to a more family-friendly environment.

PLACES TO SEE
Landmarks:

The *New York Times,* in its various guises, still dominates the area. Aside from the **original New York Times Building (44)** *(1 Times Square, W. 42nd St., Broadway/Seventh Ave.),* now most famous as the tower from which the New Year's Eve glass ball drops, there's the chateau-style **current New York Times Building (45)** *(217-247 W. 43rd St., Seventh/Eighth Aves.)* that replaced it nearby, which the *New York Times* will vacate for a fancy new skyscraper in 2007. Times Square is a cacophony of news and advertising, and no building takes it to more elegant extremes than the **NASDAQ Electronic Stock Market Building (46)** *(Broadway and 43rd St.)* and its amazing eight-story TV screen. Recently, there's been a spate of remarkable new skyscrapers in Times Square, including the **Reuters Building (47)** (*3 Times Square, NE corner of Broadway*) and the **Condé Nast Building (48)** (*4 Times Square, 42nd/43rd Sts.*), with its elegant stepped façade, home of *The New Yorker* magazine. Times Square was also famous in its day for what was known as Tin Pan Alley, or the pop music business. The center of it was the **Brill Building (50)** (*1619 Broadway at 49th St.*), where Phil Spector—among many others—worked. It's in the heart of **Music Row (51)** (*48th St., Sixth/Seventh Aves.*) where you'll find plenty of small stores selling guitars and other musical equipment. The **Time & Life Building (52)** (*1271 Sixth Ave., 50th/51st Sts.*) has one of the best public lobbies in the city, complete with works of art.

Arts & Entertainment:

Times Square is all about theater, of course, and the one with the most spectacular Beaux Arts façade is the **Lyceum Theatre (53)** (*149-157 W. 45th St., Sixth/Seventh Aves.*), which also has a great marble lined interior, complete with murals. Bette Davis and Angela Lansbury, among other stars, performed here. The **Ed Sullivan Theater (54)** (*1697-1699 Broadway, W. 53rd/W. 54th Sts.*) home to David Letterman's *Late Show,* is also a great old theater and a good place to catch stars popping in and out for the early afternoon tapings of the show. (For tickets, apply at the CBS Web site, www.cbs.com, or

visit the theater Monday-Friday, 9:30AM–12:30PM, weekends 10:00 AM–6:00 PM.) The **Winter Garden Theater (56)** (*1634-1646 Broadway, W. 50th/W. 51st Sts., www.winter garden-theater.com*) has been home to Al Jolson and the *Ziegfeld Follies* in its past, and now is best known as the place where *Cats* became Broadway's longest-running show. The **Al Hirschfeld Theater (57)** *(302-314 W. 45th St., Eighth/ Ninth Aves.)*, named after the famed *New York Times* caricaturist, has one of the most knockout interiors of all, which alone is worth the price of a ticket. Tickets for these and all other Broadway theaters are most easily purchased online from various ticket brokers, though it's possible to purchase a limited number of day-of-performance tickets from their box offices. (Note that some of these tickets are for students with appropriate ID only.) Another good place to buy day-of-performance tickets, and at discounts of up to 50%, is the **TKTS Booth (58)** *(center island of W. 47th St., Broadway/Seventh Aves., www.tdf.org)* in Duffy Square. For more information on where to buy tickets and what's on, visit the indispensable **Times Square Visitors Center (59)** *(1560 Broadway, W. 46th/W. 47th Sts., open 8:00 AM–8:00 PM daily)*. For non-theatrical entertainment, there's **Carnegie Hall (60)** *(154 W. 57th St. at Seventh Ave., 212-247-7800, www.carnegiehall.com)*, worth the pilgrimage alone to admire its handsome façade. It also has an excellent new performance space beneath it, **Zankel Hall (60)** (see Carnegie Hall Web site above for details). For great jazz, cabaret, readings, and more, there's **Town Hall (62)** *(123 W. 43rd St., Broadway/Sixth Ave., 212-997-1929, www.the-town hall-nyc.org)*. If you want something a little different, try **Madame Tussaud's New York (63)** *(234 W. 42nd St., Seventh/Eighth Aves., 800-246-8872, www.nycwax.com)*, where Ozzy Osbourne, Derek Jeter, and other waxen luminaries await. If you like **video games**, then the streets west of Times Square offer a cornucopia of such delights, though the noise can be deafening. The walk west is worth it, though, because it takes you to the pleasures of the waterfront. Not only is there the **Hudson River Park (8)** *(Hudson River to West Side Hwy., Battery Park City to 59th St.)*, with its lovely restored piers, but you can enjoy one of the great tourist pleasures: the **Circle Line (64)** *(W. 42nd St. at Pier 83, Hudson River, 212-563-3200, www.circleline42.com)*. This is a three-hour boat tour around Manhattan, passing underneath all its many bridges, with funny and knowledgeable tour guides who'll turn you into an instant Manhattan expert. Nearby is the **Intrepid Sea-Air-Space Museum (65)** *(W. 46th St. at Pier 86, Hudson River, 212-245-0072, www.intrepidmuseum.org)*, set on the massive bulk of the old *Intrepid* aircraft carrier and full of interactive amusements, two submarines, numerous jet engines, and even, floating alongside, a decommissioned Concorde aircraft. Fun for all ages.

Kids:

Times Square is now famously family- and kid-friendly since Disney moved in and forced most of the sleaze out. Some New Yorkers carp at this, but one result has been the restoration of two magnificent theaters, the **New Amsterdam Theater (66)** *(214 W. 42nd St., Seventh/Eighth Aves., www.disney.go.com/disneytheatrical/newamsterdam)* and the **New Victory Theater (67)** *(209 W. 42nd St., Seventh/Eighth Aves., 212-239-6200, www.newvictory.org)*.

The New Amsterdam is home to the eternally running smash, *The Lion King*, while the New Victory is dedicated to children's theatrical shows by visiting companies. The standard is high and any show there is well worth checking out. There's also **Madame Tussaud's (63)** *(see "Arts & Entertainment," on page 105)*, and for slightly older kids the MTV Studios (68) *(see "Where to Shop," on page 109)*. Times Square also has a gargantuan branch of Toys "R" Us (69) *(1514 Broadway, W. 44th/W. 45th Sts, 646-366-8855, www.toysrus.com)* which features a 60-foot-high Ferris wheel, a 20-foot-high T-Rex, plus a LEGO model of the Empire State Building. It's enough to satisfy any kid.

PLACES TO EAT & DRINK
Where to Eat:

If you're going to a show and in a hurry, there's always **Restaurant Row (70)** *(W. 46th St., Eighth/Ninth Aves.)*. The food is reasonable and they know you're in a rush, though there are few real surprises here. **Les Sans Culottes (71) ($$)** *(347 W. 46th St., Eighth/Ninth Aves., 212-247-4284)* is good for simple French bistro food, and **Brazil Brazil Churrascaria (72) ($)** *(328 W. 46th St., Eighth/Ninth Aves., 212-957-4300, www.brazilbrazil nyc.com)* offers tasty steaks in a bright atmosphere with a garden. There's also **Orso (73) ($$$)** *(322 W. 46th St., Eighth/Ninth Aves., 212-489-7212, www.orsorestaurant. com)* for great Italian food, one of the best places on the strip and stuffed with Broadway stars. If you have time, or if you're looking for a more relaxed post-theater meal, venture west to **Clinton** (a.k.a. "Hell's

Kitchen") *(40s and 50s west of Eighth Ave.)*, a neighborhood full of great bars and restaurants. There's **Kodama Sushi (74) ($$)** *(301 W. 45th St., Eighth/Ninth Aves., 212-582-8065)* for no-frills sushi in a no-frills space, or low-cost and delicious kosher Israeli food at **Azuri Café (75) ($)** *(465 W. 51st St., Ninth/Tenth Aves., 212-262-2920)*. Try **Le Madeleine (76) ($$$)** *(403 W. 43rd St., Ninth/Tenth Aves., 212-246-2993, www.lemadeleine. com)* for an upmarket pre-show bistro experience. **Hudson Cafeteria (77) ($$$)** *(Hudson Hotel, 356 W. 58th St., Eighth/Ninth Aves., 212-554-6000, www.hudson hotel.com/hudson_hotel_cafeteria.asp)* has amazing American fare. If you want a cheap bite on the run, there's the always reliable chain **Au Bon Pain (78) ($)** *(625 Eighth Ave., W. 40th/W. 41st Sts., 212-502-4823, www.aubonpain.com)*.

Bars & Nightlife:

ESPN Zone (79) *(1472 Broadway at 42nd St., 212-921-3776, www.espnzone.com)* is huge, full of massive TV screens all showing sports, and it offers fast food and beer. If that's your idea of fun, this is a paradise made for you. **Garvey's (80)** *(270 W. 45th St, at Eighth Ave., 212-997-6400)* is a perfect place for a quick pre-show drink; it's unpretentious, friendly, and doesn't pretend to offer more than pub-grub basics and good beer. **Show (81)** *(135 W. 41st. St., Sixth Ave./Broadway, 212-278-0988)* is a club to please both men and women looking for a little light-hearted sleaze, with male and female performers who will dance for your personal pleasure. It's cozy, sexy, and surprisingly still legal in the new squeaky clean Times Square.

WHERE TO SHOP

Times Square and its environs is not the most restful area to shop, but there are a few places that are uniquely New York and worth a visit. The MTV Store (68) *(1515 Broadway at W. 44th St., 212-846-5654)*, located beneath its broadcast studios, is a haven for the pop-culture addicted with a wide variety of MTV-related merchandise, videos and DVDs, plus the real draw—signings and appearances by musicians and MTV presenters. The Virgin Megastore (82) *(1540 Broadway, W. 45th/W. 46th Sts., 212-921-1020, www.virginmega.com)* does indeed live up to its name, being extremely mega and offering numerous listening booths as well in which to check out the merchandise. Visit its Web site for details of upcoming in-store appearances.

WHERE TO STAY

Staying at the New York Marriott Marquis Times Square (83) ($$) *(1535 Broadway, W. 45th/W. 46th Sts., 212-398-1900, www.nymarriottmarquis.com)* hardly feels like being in New York at all, with its L.A.-style valet parking at street level (you have to take an elevator up to reception), and its dizzying James Bond-style central atrium rising 49 floors; however, it's a real trip staying here, and the views from its revolving bar/restaurant are amazing. The Muse (84) ($$$) *(130 W. 46th St., Sixth/Seventh Aves., 212-485-2400, www.themusehotel.com)* may cost a bit, but this is a luxury place that will cosset you perfectly. If you're here for the theater, there's no more convenient place to stay.

chapter 5

FLATIRON DISTRICT & GRAMERCY
MIDTOWN & MURRAY HILL

FLATIRON DISTRICT & GRAMERCY MIDTOWN & MURRAY HILL

Places to See:

4. Empire State Building
5. Chrysler Building
6. Rockefeller Center
7. NBC
8. St. Patrick's Cathedral
9. Lever House
10. Seagram Building
11. Bryant Park
12. New York Public Library
13. Grand Central Terminal
14. Tudor City
15. United Nations Headquarters
16. The Ford Foundation Building
17. Museum of Modern Art
18. American Folk Art Museum
19. Museum of Television and Radio
20. Museum of Arts & Design
21. Sony Wonder Technology Lab
22. FAO Schwarz
49. Madison Square Park
50. Flatiron Building
51. New York Life Insurance Company Building
52. The Players
53. National Arts Club
54. Theodore Roosevelt Birthplace
55. 69th Regiment Armory
56. Morgan Library
57. Augustus Saint-Gaudens Park
78. Radio City Music Hall

Places to Eat & Drink:

23. Burger Heaven
24. Dishes
25. Cosi
26. Alcala
27. Morton's, The Steakhouse
28. Aquavit
29. Guastavino's
30. Delegates' Dining Room
31. The King Cole Bar at the St. Regis Hotel
32. Oak Room at the Algonquin Hotel
33. P. J. Clarke's
34. The Campbell Apartment
35. Club Vue
36. Whiskey Blue
37. Bill's Gay Nineties
38. Artisanal
39. Les Halles

FLATIRON DISTRICT & GRAMERCY

F **V** to 14th St. or 23rd St.; **L** **N** **Q** **R** **W** **4** **5** **6** to 14th St.-Union Square; **6** to 23rd St. or 28th St.; **N** **R** **W** to 23rd St. or 28th St.

⊛ SNAPSHOT ⊛

Today, these districts are alike in both being highly "respectable," thriving neighborhoods, full of shops and museums. However, not so long ago the Flatiron District (roughly 14th to 29th streets between Fifth and Park avenues), and its main public space, Madison Square Park, was a raggedy, crime-ridden sister to neighboring Gramercy Park, which had largely retained its slumbering sense of wealthy calm since the 19th century. A huge face-lift to Madison Square Park and the surrounding areas put an end to this disparity, and now both are essential places on any visitor's itinerary.

PLACES TO SEE
Landmarks:

Like Union Square Park nearby, **Madison Square Park (49)** *(23rd to 26th Sts., Fifth Ave. to Madison Ave.)* has recently seen a reversal of fortune from a drug-plagued place to one where crowds sit, eating lunch during the day, or looking at art exhibits and listening to music on summer nights, thanks to the efforts of the Madison Square Park conservancy *(www.madisonsquarepark.org*

for details). The park has several claims to fame, first as the likely site of the country's first baseball team, the New York Knickerbockers, founded by Alexander Cartwright in 1845, and also as the site of the original Madison Square Garden, long since transferred north to its current site above Penn Station. The two most notable buildings are the **Flatiron Building (50)** *(175 Fifth Ave., 22nd/23rd Sts.)*, which gives the neighborhood its name, and the **New York Life Insurance Company Building (51)** *(51 Madison Ave., 26th/27th Sts.)*. A gorgeous wedge-shaped 22-story slice of Renaissance terracotta completed in 1903, the Flatiron Building gained its name because it was shaped like a clothing iron. At the time, the building's high-rise steel structure was innovative and it became an instant landmark at the northern end of what was known as "Ladies Mile," the city's most important shopping area. The other great neighborhood edifice, the **New York Life Insurance Company Building (51)** was designed by Cass Gilbert, the same architect who built the Woolworth Building. This lovely 40-story limestone building was built on the site of the original Madison Square Garden. Gramercy Park—unlike Madison Square Park's open-to-all democracy—is based on the English form of a private garden in the center of a square and is only open to residents who have a key, an infinitely prized status object among local residents. Just because you can't get in doesn't mean you shouldn't gaze at the surrounding buildings: there's **The Players (52)** *(16 Gramercy Park S., Park Ave. S./Irving Pl., www.theplayersnyc.org)*, a beautiful Greek Revival town house once owned by famous actor Edwin Booth (his brother shot Lincoln). It is now a private club for men and women in the arts and business. Next door is another famous club, the **National Arts Club (53)** *(15 Gramercy Park S., www.nationalartsclub. org)*, in Gothic Revival style, where in a suitable boozy atmosphere artists and writers still disport themselves amid walls displaying their art.

Arts & Entertainment:

If you like your museums dimly lit and uncrowded, the wonderful **Theodore Roosevelt Birthplace (54)** *(28 E. 20th St., Broadway/Park Ave. S., 212-260-1616, cash only, www.theodore-roosevelt.com/trbirthplace.html)* is for you. Because it's a national historic site (though the original building was demolished in 1916), uniformed Federal Rangers stand guard suspiciously as you peer at the brown furniture and fusty trophy room. Much more modern, at least in spirit, is the **69th Regiment Armory (55)** *(68 Lexington Ave., E. 25th/E. 26th Sts., 212-988-4099)*, host to the original 1913 Armory Show where cubism and other shocking European phenomena were first unveiled for the American public. Its vast 27,000 square-foot space is host to a number of important arts and antiques fairs during the year.

Kids:

This isn't the most child-friendly of Manhattan neighborhoods, but there's a lovely playground in the Gramercy Park area called the **Augustus Saint-Gaudens Park (57)** *(19th St. at Second Ave.)*, and the **Comfort Diner (58)** *(25 W. 23rd St., Fifth/Sixth Aves., 212-741-1010)* offers special kids' meals, booster seats, and an understanding waitstaff. Whether you're an adult or a kid, you'll love Books of Wonder (77) *(18 W. 18th St., Fifth/Sixth Aves., 212-989-3270, www.booksofwonder. net)*, which stocks childhood classics from *Winnie the Pooh* to *Harry Potter*. It also offers frequent author readings and signings.

PLACES TO EAT & DRINK
Where to Eat:

Craft (60) ($$$) *(43 E. 19th St., Broadway/Park Ave. S., 212-780-0880, www.craftrestaurant.com)* is an amazingly minimalist space with simple food—including terrific desserts. **City Bakery (61) ($)** *(3 W. 18th St., Fifth/Sixth Aves., 212-366-1414)* is a neighborhood standard with a great buffet and even better cakes and pastries. If you're in Madison Square Park, don't miss **Shake Shack (62) ($)** *(S. Side Park, near Madison Ave./23rd St., 212-889-6600, www.shakeshacknyc.com)*, where you can recover from sightseeing with a hot dog, burger, or ice cream. Over at **dévi (63) ($$)** *(8 E. 18th St., Broadway/Fifth Ave., 212-691-1300)* there's wonderful Indian food served in a brightly lit, colorful atmosphere. French bistro **L'Express (64) ($$)** *(249 Park Ave. S. at 20th St., 212-254-5858)* is a locals' favorite, open 24 hours a day, and for something

a little more adventurous (and costly) there's **SushiSamba (65) ($$$)** *(245 Park Ave. S., 19th/20th Sts., 212-475-9377, www.sushi samba.com)*, a Japanese-South American fusion restaurant that also serves killer cocktails. For tasty sandwiches and delicious baked goods, try **71 Irving Place (75) ($$)** *(71 Irving Place, E. 18th/19th Sts., 212-995-5252).*

Bars & Nightlife:

The **Rodeo Bar (66)** *(375 Third Ave. at 27th St., 212-683-6500, www.rodeobar.com)* has a real roadhouse feel to it, complete with country music and sawdust on the floor. It's noisy, has great live music, and if that's your scene you'll love it. **The Cutting Room (67)** *(19 W. 24th St., Broadway/Sixth Ave., 212-691-1900, www.thecuttingroomnyc.com)* is a stylish venue with great live music, especially jazz, and a bar upfront where you're quite likely to encounter celebs pretending they're just ordinary folk.

WHERE TO SHOP

Like the raffish English gent look? You can't go wrong shopping at Paul Smith (68) *(108 Fifth Ave. at 16th St., 212-627-9770, www.paulsmith.co.uk).* Smith's tailored suits, famous striped socks and shirts, and super-cool shoes can't be beat. If your budget won't stretch that far, there's the excellent 17 at 17 Thrift Shop (69) *(17 W. 17th St., Fifth/Sixth Aves., 212-727-7516, www.ujafedny.org),* where all sorts of bargains on clothes to bric-a-brac can be found. If you're a music lover, Academy Records (70) *(12 W. 18th St., Fifth/Sixth Aves., 212-242-3000, www.academyrecords.com)* has an amazing jazz and classical collection in both vinyl and CD format in a browser-friendly environment. Don't worry about the weird name—Fishs Eddy (71) *(889 Broadway at E. 19th St.,*

212-420-9020, www.fishseddy.com) is a mini-chain that offers irresistible china and glassware from over-stocked corporations, factories, and out-of-business restaurants. Each plate tells a story. And it's cheap—you'll walk out with twice what you expected to buy. Camera buffs have plenty of places in NYC, but Alkit Pro Camera (72) *(222 Park Ave. S. at 18th St., 212-674-1515, www.alkit.com),* with its choice of NYC locations, is among the best. You'll be treated like a pro even if you aren't one. ABC Carpet & Home (76) *(888 Broadway at E. 19th St., 212-473-3000, www.abc home.com)* is famous for its huge selection of home furnishings, decorations, and bazaar-like atmosphere.

WHERE TO STAY

At around $139 for a double room per night, with private bathrooms, and with amenities such as cable and Internet hookup, the Murray Hill Inn (73) ($) *(143 E. 30th St., Lexington/Third Aves., 212-683-6900, www. murrayhillinn.com)* is a steal. Hotel 31 (74) ($-$$) *(120 E. 31st St., Park Ave. S./Lexington Ave., 212-685-3060, www.hotel31.com)* is grungier, but at around $85 a night and up, it's hard to complain. The Union Square Inn (59) ($) *(209 E. 14th St., Second/Third Aves., 212-614-0500, www.unionsquareinn.com)* is part of a mini-chain of good and basic hotels scattered around prime sites in the city, though their popularity means some of them can be hard to get into at times.

MIDTOWN & MURRAY HILL

Ⓑ Ⓓ Ⓕ Ⓥ to 42nd St.-Bryant Park or
47th-50th Sts.-Rockefeller Center; Ⓢ ④ ⑤ ⑥ Ⓐ to
Grand Central-42nd St.; Ⓝ Ⓡ Ⓦ to Fifth Ave.-59th St.;
Ⓔ to Fifth Ave.-53rd St.)

◦ SNAPSHOT ◦

When visitors think of New York, the first images that
come to mind are usually the iconic ones of its famous
skyscrapers, in all their Deco glory, rising high above the
bustling streets. This is Midtown, the place that for
many—New Yorkers and tourists alike—epitomizes the
city. It's here that Fifth Avenue swells to its most majestic state. The Empire State Building, Chrysler Building,
Rockefeller Center, and United Nations complex, to
name just a few, ascend skywards, and Radio City Music
Hall, Tiffany's, the Plaza Hotel, Saks, and a host of other
New York institutions made familiar through a million
TV shows and movies, can be found here. It's no wonder that a first-time visitor's impression is
often: *Haven't I seen all this before?* Murray
Hill, a highly fashionable residential area in
lower Midtown, contains some remarkable
buildings (in particular a number of lovely
carriage houses now converted to residences), as well as restaurants and shops.
It's not quite as electric as Midtown (what
is?), but it's a pleasant and rewarding

neighborhood to venture into if you wish to lower the street energy for a while.

PLACES TO SEE
Landmarks:

Perhaps the most famous address in the world, **Fifth Avenue** was originally a residential street for the ultra-wealthy, before becoming one of the city's most prestigious commercial strips as the big stores began to move north from 34th Street. Some of the original private mansions were later converted into shops. Cartier Inc. (2) *(Fifth Ave. at 52nd St., 212-753-0111, www.cartier. com)*, the jewelers, now occupies one of the greatest Renaissance mansions on Fifth Avenue; and Versace (3) *(647 Fifth Ave., 51st/52nd Sts., 212-317-0224)* occupies a former Vanderbilt mansion next door. Skyscrapers are what the neighborhood is famous for, and the **Empire State Building (4)** *(350 Fifth Ave., 33rd/34th Sts., 212-736-3100, www.esbnyc.com)* is the most famous of all. At 1,250 feet, it beat out the spanking new Chrysler

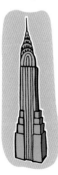

Building for crown of tallest building in the world when it opened in 1931. The sights from its 86th floor viewing level are amazing. (Note that with new security measures, it can take *a long time* to get up there.) It may be a touch shorter, but the **Chrysler Building (5)** *(405 Lexington Ave., 42nd/43rd Sts.)*, with its great gargoyles and Deco detailing, is far more romantic and has an infinitely richer public lobby. **Rockefeller Center (6)** *(Fifth to Sixth Aves., 48th/51st Sts.,*

212-632-3975, www.rockefellercenter.com) is a collection of 19 buildings—both office and commercial space—a sunken shopping plaza, and an open-air public plaza, all brilliantly arranged in harmony with each other. Work began in the 1930s and was extended until the early 1950s. **NBC (7)** *(30 Rockefeller Plaza, 49th St., Fifth/Sixth Aves., call 212-664-3700 for tour info, www.nbc.com)* is a tenant. There's also good shopping *(see "Where to Shop," on page 129)* in the plaza above and below, and a wonderful **Rink at Rockefeller Center** for ice-skating, open October to April *(call 212-332-7654 for prices and times)*. Rockefeller Plaza is the site of New York City's Christmas tree and its celebrity lighting each year. On a less secular level, there's **St. Patrick's Cathedral (8)** *(Fifth Ave., E. 50th/E. 51st Sts., www.ny-archdiocese.org)* nearby, a Gothic masterpiece where the hush once inside its vast doors makes a lovely contrast to the perpetual bustle outside. **Radio City Music Hall (78)** *(1260 Sixth Ave., W. 50th/W. 51st Sts., 212-247-4777, www.radiocity.com)* remains one of the great architectural and theatrical gems of the city. Today, it's best known for its annual Christmas extravaganza with the high kickin' Rockettes. You can take in its sumptuous interior, without paying for a show, by joining one of its regular behind-the-scenes tours. If you like your architecture modern, a little farther north is the famous **Lever House (9)** *(390 Park Ave., E. 53rd/E. 54th Sts.)*—an

International Style stainless steel and glass curtain-walled office building that inspired a million knockoffs. The other classic International Style skyscraper is the **Seagram Building (10)** *(375 Park Ave., E. 52nd/E. 53rd Sts.)*, a sleek, almost ominous, glass and bronze-framed tower designed by Mies van der Rohe and Philip Johnson. Between West 40th and West 42nd streets on the east side of Sixth Avenue lies **Bryant Park (11)** *(www.bryantpark.org)*, one of the loveliest public spaces in the city. In warm weather you can pull up a chair and sit on the graveled walkways pretending you're in the Tuileries. The park is behind the majestic **New York Public Library (12)** *(476 Fifth Avenue, W. 42nd to 40th Sts., www.nypl.org)*, a Beaux Arts masterpiece with its famous twin lions guarding the entrance. The Rose Reading room is worth a visit, and there are usually excellent free exhibitions, too. Eastward lies **Grand Central Terminal (13)** *(E. 42nd to E. 44th Sts., Vanderbilt to Lexington Aves., 212-340-2583, www.grandcentral terminal.com)*, one of New York's greatest landmarks, now beautifully restored inside. Check out its famous painted ceiling of the constellations. As part of the restoration, there's also a terrific (but expensive) food market on the main level and a (much cheaper) food

court on the lower level *(see "Where to Shop," on page 129, and "Where to Eat & Drink," on page 126)*. Head toward the East River and you'll encounter **Tudor City (14)** *(E. 40th St. to E. 43rd St., First/Second Aves., www.tudorcity.com)*, a fascinating

1920s Tudor-style collection of apartment buildings funded by Rockefeller alongside what was once the city's busiest slaughterhouse area. They form an enclave of peace and quiet from busy Second Avenue, and nestling in the middle is a delightful and beautifully maintained public park. Nearby, in high-modern style lies the **United Nations Headquarters (15)** *(E. 42nd to E. 48th Sts., First Ave./FDR Drive, 212-963-8687 for tour info, www.un.org),* where you technically leave U.S. soil as you enter. **The Ford Foundation Building (16)** *(321 E. 42nd St., First/Second Aves.),* with its incredible atrium that is visible from both the street and offices, is arguably the finest postwar building in New York. It's one of the great public spaces in the city and you just know it costs a bundle to keep all those delicate trees alive.

Arts & Entertainment:

Midtown has some excellent museums, including the newly renovated and expanded **Museum of Modern Art (MoMA) (17)** *(11 W. 53rd St., Fifth/Sixth Aves., 212-708-9400, www.moma.org).* Its white walls and pure spaces are home to a permanent collection by the likes of Matisse, Picasso, Pollock, and Warhol, and it features major exhibitions as well. It's a whopping $20 for admission, but few complain once they've seen what's inside. It also has arguably the best gift shop of any museum in the city. Less famous is the **American Folk Art Museum (18)** *(45 W. 53rd St., Fifth/Sixth Aves., 212-265-1040, www.folkartmuseum.org),* housing a delightful collection of early Americana, paintings, signboards, quilts, and the like, as well as temporary exhibitions.

And its magnificent award-winning bronze-plated façade makes it equally as deserving of all the hyperbole lavished on the new MoMA. The **Museum of Television and Radio (19)** *(25 W. 52nd St., Fifth/Sixth Aves., 212-621-6800, www.mtr.org)* provides curated shows on particular themes such as Hollywood or an individual performer, as well as artifacts and screenings from all ages of the American entertainment industry. *(See also in "Kids" below.)* The **Museum of Arts & Design (20)** *(40 W. 53rd St., Fifth/Sixth Aves., 212-956-3535, www.americancraft museum.org)* offers an eclectic array of exhibitions and permanent exhibits reflecting all forms of media—from painting and sculpture to video, neon, and even origami. It also has a great series of kids' programs. *(See "Kids," below.)* The venerable **Morgan Library (56)** *(29 E. 36th St., Fifth/Madison Aves., 212-685-0610, www. morganlibrary.org)* was the original home of the uber-robber baron, financier J. P. Morgan, and along with his magnificent library, you can see Morgan's jaw-dropping collection of Italian Renaissance paintings and sculpture.

Kids:

The **Museum of Television and Radio (19)** *(see "Arts & Entertainment," above)* offers a wonderful series of workshops entitled "Recreating Radio" *(call 212-621-6674, for details),* in which kids, aged nine and up, collaborate to make an old-fashioned radio serial program, complete with scripts, sound effects, and editing. Afterwards, they get to take away a recording of their labors. The **Museum of Arts & Design (20)** *(see above for more)* also offers kids' programs, including one in which participants get to try out a different medium each week—such as wood, glass, fiber, and metal. For the tech-enthusiast among your kids, you can't beat the **Sony Wonder Technology Lab (21)** *(56th St. at Madison Ave., 212-833-8100, www.sony wondertechlab.com)*—four floors of interactive fun, including a 73-seat HDTV viewing theater, where you and your kids can make music, video, and film clips, explore computers, and much more. If your little darlings are demanding toys, sate 'em at **FAO Schwarz (22)** *(767 Fifth Ave., 58th/59th Sts., 212-644-9400)*, a vast palace of toys, recently restored and utterly addictive to any child.

PLACES TO EAT & DRINK
Where to Eat:

For a quick and cheap burger fix, there's **Burger Heaven (23) ($)** *(20 E. 49th St., Fifth/Madison Aves., 212-755-2166)*—rushed, but tasty. For sandwiches, soups, and salads (weekdays only) that are heads and shoulders above the average, **Dishes (24) ($)** *(6 E. 45th St., Fifth/ Madison Aves., 212-687-5511)* is the place to go. The **Cosi (25) ($)** *(60 E. 56th St., Madison/Park Aves., 212-588-1225)* chain of sandwich shops is also a good cheap bet. If you want to splurge more and you like tapas and Basque food, **Alcala (26) ($$)** *(342 E. 46th St., First/ Second Aves., 212-370-1866)* is excellent. For a serious carnivorous session, **Morton's, The Steakhouse (27) ($$$)** *(551 Fifth Ave. at 45th St., 212-972-3315, www.mortons. com)* can't be beat. Scandinavian food is on the rare side in New York, but **Aquavit (28) ($$$)** *(65 E. 55th St., Madison/Park Aves., 212-307-7311, www.aquavit.org)*

wows even jaded city palates. If you're happy to enjoy a magnificent space rather than the greatest of cuisine, Terence Conran's **Guastavino's (29) ($$$)** *(409 E. 59th St., First/York Aves., 212-980-2455, www.guastavinos.com)* is set in a vast tiled and vaulted ceiling inside the arches of the 59th Street Bridge and will leave you gaping. The **Delegates' Dining Room (30) ($$)** *(UN, 4th floor, First Ave. at 46th St., 212-963-7626)* at the United Nations has the most eclectic clientele by far of any restaurant in the city, and offers amazing river views with its weekday-only lunch buffets. You're advised to reserve. Finally, Grand Central Terminal is home to the **Grand Central Oyster Bar (13) ($$)** *(see Grand Central Terminal in "Landmarks," on page 122, www.oysterbarny.com)* in its lower level, where you can pig out on oysters and clam chowder in an elegant and truly iconic New York City space. The lower level food court also has a large array of cheaper fast food options.

Bars & Nightlife:

The King Cole Bar at the St. Regis Hotel (31) *(2 E. 55th St., Fifth/Madison Aves., 212-339-6721, www.starwood hotels.com)* is *waaay* expensive, but the clubby armchairs, wooden paneling, and Maxfield Parrish mural behind the bar of King Cole himself make it worth every cent. Just as pricey is the **Oak Room at the Algonquin Hotel (32)** *(59 W. 44th St., Fifth/Sixth Aves., 212-840-6800, www.algonquinhotel.com)*, where there's great jazz and a darkened atmosphere. As dark and historic as these two but far more democratic, **P. J. Clarke's (33)** *(915 Third Ave at 55th St., 212-317-1616,* *www.pjclarkes.com)* offers beer, music, and comfort food. **The Campbell Apartment (34)** *(15 Vanderbilt Ave., 42nd/43rd Sts., 212-953-0409)* is a 1920s-era section of Grand Central Terminal, complete with 25-foot-high ceilings, that serves up jazz, cocktails, and a general Deco sensibility. Brutally modern, with its techno and hip-hop sound track, plus digital state-of-the-art sound system and 360-degree cinema screen, **Club Vue (35)** *(151 E. 50th St., Lexington/Third Aves., 212-753-1144)* offers an entirely different scene. For unashamed hipsters there's **Whiskey Blue (36)** *(541 Lexington Ave. at 49th St., 212-407-2947)*, part of the trendy W Hotel. For unabashed nostalgia lovers there's **Bill's Gay Nineties (37)** *(57 E. 54th St., Madison/Park Aves., 212-355-0243)*, a piano bar that began life as a speakeasy in 1930. In Murray Hill, **Artisanal (38)** *(2 Park Ave. at 32nd St., 212-725-8585)* is a great bar and restaurant where cheese and wine rule. The folks here are serious about their tasting pleasures, and will help you find just the right fromage to go with that special glass of wine. If you're a foodie, this place is a must. **Les Halles (39)** *(411 Park Ave. South, E. 28th/E. 29th St., 212-679-4111, www.leshalles.net)* is celeb chef Anthony Bourdain's famous bar/restaurant, where a slick and well-heeled crowd tuck into brasserie food with gusto. If you want a more casual experience here, simply sit at the bar with a drink and enjoy the excellent people-watching. **Joshua Tree (40)** *(513 Third Ave., E. 34th/E. 35th Sts., 212-689-0058)* is a neighborhood institution for no particular reason other than that it's simply there. But it's a good and friendly place to drop by for a beer or two, and its young crowd is both well-educated and easy on the eye.

WHERE TO SHOP

A landmark since 1902, Saks Fifth Avenue (41) *(611 Fifth Ave. at 50th St., 212-753-4000, www.saks.com)* is one of the greatest of all New York's department stores and it's great for men's and women's clothes, jewelry, perfumes, and gifts. Call for details of its regular trunk shows. Just as smart is Bergdorf Goodman (42) *(754 Fifth Ave., 57th/58th Sts., 212-753-7300, www.bergdorfgoodman. com)*, where you'll see fur-coated ladies who lunch while checking out the jewelry and shoes. Prices are steep, though the seasonal sales offer genuine bargains. Think you can't afford something at Tiffany & Co. (1) *(727 Fifth Ave, 56th/57th Sts., 212-755-8000, www.tiffany.com)*? Well, there are a few things the average purse can handle, including a silver bookmark (in that quintessential little blue box), and a few other items "under $175," as its Web site puts it. For high fashion there's Gucci (43) *(685 Fifth Ave., at 54th St., 212-826-2600, www.gucci. com)*, a place where you will either feel entirely at home

 or run screaming through the door, depending on your tastes. At Chanel (44) *(15 E. 57th St., Fifth/Madison Aves., 212-355-5050, www.chanel.com)* you can pick up a lipstick for a mere $20, or a suit for $2,000 and up. If you just want good, honest, no-nonsense, relatively inexpensive men's clothes there's always Brooks Brothers (45) *(666 Fifth*

Ave. at W. 53rd St., 212-261-9440, www.brooksbrothers.com). For literary types there's **Bauman Rare Books (46)** *(535 Madison Ave., 54th/55th Sts., 212-751-0011, www.baumanrarebooks.com),* where first editions rule and you can ogle such beautiful bound editions as an original *Alice in Wonderland* or Darwin's *Origin of the Species.* For food, there's **Grand Central Terminal Food Market (13)** *(see Grand Central Terminal in "Landmarks," on page 122),* which has great delectables, particularly its meat, fish, and selection of fabulous cheese, as well as gift items such as chocolates and flowers. The lower level of **Rockefeller Center (6)** *(see Rockefeller Center in "Landmarks," on page 120)* offers a whole range of gifts and clothes, from smart designer apparel to basic tee shirts and jeans.

WHERE TO STAY

Money no object? You can't beat the **Waldorf-Astoria Hotel (47) ($$$)** *(301 Park Ave., at 50th St., 212-355-3100, www.waldorfastoria.com)*—a Deco masterpiece where Frank Sinatra, Diana Ross, and a host of other well-known performers have entertained diners. The lobby's worth a look even if you aren't staying there. A much more reasonable option is the **Pickwick Arms (48) ($)** *(230 E. 51st St., Second/Third Aves., 212-355-0300, www.pickwickarms.com)*—a real steal at around $120 a night, with shared bathrooms for a number of rooms.

chapter 6

LINCOLN CENTER & ENVIRONS UPPER WEST SIDE

Places to See:

1. Lincoln Center for the Performing Arts
1. Metropolitan Opera House
1. New York State Theater
1. Walter Reade Theater
1. Film Society of Lincoln Center
2. Time Warner Center
3. Columbus Circle
4. Gallery of Modern Art
20. Ansonia Hotel
21. Central Park West
22. The Dakota
23. San Remo Apartments
24. Congregation Shearith Israel
25. Pomander Walk
26. Riverside Drive
27. Riverside Park
28. West 79th Street Marina and Boat Basin
29. Merkin Concert Hall
30. Frederick P. Rose Hall
31. American Museum of Natural History/ Rose Center for Earth and Space
32. Beacon Theatre
33. Symphony Space
34. El Taller Latino Americano
35. Makor
36. Children's Museum of Manhattan
37. Penny Whistle Toys
47. Dizzy's Club *Coca-Cola*

Places to Eat & Drink:

6. Big Nick's Burger & Pizza Joint
7. Rosa Mexicano
8. Ollie's
9. Sapphire Indian Cuisine
10. Stone Rose Lounge
11. Gabriel's Bar
12. Vince & Eddie's
38. Café Lalo
39. Alice's Tea Cup
40. Boat Basin Café
41. Café Luxembourg
42. Gray's Papaya
43. Assaggio
44. Jean-Luc
45. Carmine's
46. Sipan
48. Compass
49. Sugar Bar
50. Ruby Foo's

51. Nice Matin
60. Abbey Pub

57. Robert Marc
58. Maxilla & Mandible

Where to Shop:

Where to Stay:

LINCOLN CENTER & ENVIRONS

1 *to 66th St.-Lincoln Center;*
A C B D 1 *to 59th St.-Columbus Circle*

SNAPSHOT

The neighborhood around the Lincoln Center for the Performing Arts was originally part of Clinton, its neighbor to the south. Both areas were collectively known as "Hell's Kitchen," a vital, working-class neighborhood that sprawled westward to the Hudson and was infamous for its gangs and crime. Then in the early 1960s gentrification arrived in the newly minted form of "urban renewal," and the crumbling brownstones filled with lonely studios were converted back to family use again or demolished in great swaths to make way for—among other things—places such as Lincoln Center. The site is filled with venues, including the Metropolitan Opera House, New York State Theater, and the Avery Fisher Hall. Individually they're a fairly loveless group of buildings, but their saving grace is the wonderful main public plaza that unites them, and on a summer's night when the fountains are flowing there's no more magical spot to be in New York.

PLACES TO SEE
Landmarks:
Lincoln Center for the Performing Arts (1) *(W. 62nd to W. 66th Sts., Columbus/Amsterdam Aves., 212-546-2656 for event listings, www.lincolncenter.org)* is most impressive at night, when the buildings and fountain are all lit up—it's a fun spot to just hang out and watch New York's ceaseless street parade. In the summer there's dancing in the plaza (see "Midsummer Night Swing" on its Web site). For individual attractions, see "Arts & Entertainment," page 135. The other major landmark here is the spanking new **Time Warner Center (2)** *(SW side of Columbus Circle., 58th/59th Sts., www.timewarner. com)*, a twin-towered glass monolith that rises far above everything else. Inside its shiny 2.8-million square foot, $1.7-billion interior is a mini-city in itself, consisting of a hotel, condos, shops, restaurants, corporate headquarters, and more. *(See "Where to Shop," "Where to Eat & Drink," and "Arts & Entertainment.")* Everyone agreed that Columbus Circle needed a new building that would make a statement and help define this awkward circle-in-a-grid space, but its glossy opulence tends to polarize opinion: you'll either love it or hate it. Dwarfed

by this new building is the statue of Columbus perched on his column in the center of **Columbus Circle (3)**, hand on hip as though in defiance at all that's going on around him. On the far side of Columbus Circle is the "lollipop building," a much excoriated and also much-loved white marble building originally designed as the **Gallery of Modern Art (4)** *(2 Columbus Circle, Broadway/Eighth Ave.)* for A & P supermarket heir Huntington Hartford. It's had a checkered past and now stands empty. Plans are afoot to either knock it down or at least alter its façade drastically. You can't explore New York without encountering mega-developer Donald Trump's influence. A few years ago he took over the old 44-story Gulf and Western building, had it re-clad at vast expense by architect Philip Johnson, and—voila!—the **Trump International Hotel & Tower (5)** *(1 Central Park West at Columbus Circle, 212-299-1000, www.trumpintl.com)* was born. The building is home to supermodels and baseball players, and anyone else who can afford the rent.

Arts & Entertainment:

Lincoln Center (1) *(see "Landmarks," on page 134)* is New York's altar of high culture, and whether it's ballet, opera, symphonic music, or film, you'll find it here at its finest. The **Metropolitan Opera House (1)** *(212-362-6000, www.metopera.org)* is the flashiest Lincoln Center building, located right in front of the plaza's main fountain, and offers a wide range of operas—from *Tosca* and *La Boheme*, that an operatic novice will enjoy, to more esoteric fare. It has an excellent and informative Web site. The Met's own company is in residence September through May, and touring companies perform in the summer. The **New York State Theater (1)** houses the **New York City Ballet** *(www.nycballet.com, 212-870-5570)* and the **New York City Opera** *(www.nycopera.com),* which is cheaper than the Met, and offers the opportunity to spot rising talent in the making before they become more expensive to catch. The **Walter Reade Theater (1)** *(212-875-5600, www.filmlinc.com, cash only at the box office)* is home to the **Film Society of Lincoln Center (1)**, which sponsors the annual New York Film festival, as well as offering year-round viewings of films not otherwise available, plus revivals and directors' talks. A block away from all this high-brow activity is the excellent and quirky **Merkin Concert Hall (29)** *(Kaufman Center, 129 W. 67th St., Broadway/Amsterdam Ave., 212-501-3330, www.kaufman-center.org)*, which features jazz, experimental music, live broadcasts, and family theater matinees. **Makor (35)** *(35 W. 67th St., CPW/Columbus Ave., 212-601-1000, www.makor.org)* also offers a wide range of somewhat lighter and more eclectic fare than the Lincoln Center, including film, spoken word, theater, and musical events in its basement setting. The **Time Warner Center (2)** *(see "Landmarks," on page 134)* has several cultural hot spots, most notably the **Frederick P. Rose Hall (30)** *(Broadway at 60th St., 5th floor, 212-258-9800, www.jazzatlincolncenter.com)*, a stunning glass-backed auditorium with amazing acoustics and sweeping views of Manhattan in the background. It hosts Lincoln Center's annual Jazz Festival, among other events. **Dizzy's Club *Coca-Cola* (47)** *(www.jazzatlincoln center.com)* is a more intimate retro-style jazz club, also on the fifth floor, that holds just 140 people.

Kids:

Lincoln Center (1) *(www.lincolncenter.org)* has a number of great activities for kids, especially outdoor events in the summer. Check out the "Just for Kids" section on its Web site. Most of the eating places around Lincoln Center are pretty adult-oriented, but a few blocks north there's the loud and very fabulous **Big Nick's Burger & Pizza Joint (6) ($)** *(70 W. 71 St. at Columbus Ave., 212-799-4450)*. The name says it all.

PLACES TO EAT & DRINK
Where to Eat:

There's a cluster of restaurants and watering holes in the **Time Warner Center (2)** *(see "Landmarks," on page 134)*, including **Per Se (2) ($$$)** *(4th floor, 212-823-9335, www.perseny.com)*, ace chef Thomas Keller's new joint, which currently has about a two-month waiting list but which is, according to the chosen few who've gained entry, the best restaurant in New York. Lincoln Center is, of course, surrounded by restaurants, and **Rosa Mexicano (7) ($$$)** *(61 Columbus Ave. at W. 62nd St., 212-977-7700, www.rosamexicano.com)* offers fantastic Mexican food and great drinks. On the cheaper side, try **Ollie's (8) ($)** *(1991 Broadway, W. 67th/W. 68th Sts., 212-595-8181)* for fast yet tasty Chinese food. For a calmer environment than most around here, there's **Sapphire Indian Cuisine (9) ($$)** *(1845 Broadway, W. 60th/W. 61st Sts., 212-245-4444)*, which also offers a great low-cost lunch.

Bars & Nightlife:

The **Time Warner Center (2)** *(see "Landmarks," on page 134)* offers a number of night life opportunities, the fanciest being Rande Gerber's **Stone Rose Lounge (10)**

(10 Columbus Circle, 4th floor, 212-823-9769). The views of Central Park at night are pretty cool, and who knows—you may even bump into some celebrities. **Gabriel's Bar (11)** *(11 W. 60th St., Columbus Ave./Broadway, 212-956-4600, www.gabrielsbarandrest. com)* is a no-pretense Italian restaurant, with wonderful cozy booths in which to pull up at night for a few post-show drinks. **Vince & Eddie's (12)** *(70 W. 68th St., Columbus Ave./Central Park West, 212-721-0068)* is another restaurant that's great for drinks, and has a secret garden and romantic fireplaces. There's live classical music on the weekends.

WHERE TO SHOP

The **Time Warner Center (2)** *(see "Landmarks," on page 134)* has a collection of high-class stores, if money is no object, including menswear designer Joseph Abboud's new flagship store. For lesser mortals there's always J. Crew, Coach, Williams-Sonoma, and the like. The Whole Foods supermarket here is the largest in New York, 59,000 square feet of impeccably displayed and carefully chosen goods, along with a cafe and a sushi bar. If you love beauty products, the

Sephora (13) *(10 Columbus Circle, SW side, 212-823-9383, www.sephora. com)* chain has a small branch here offering Pop, Stila, and other cosmetic brands with unusually friendly service for a beauty joint. For household items there's two trusty stalwarts nearby, **Pottery Barn (14)** *(1965 Broadway*

at W. 67th St., 212-579-8477, www.
potterybarn.com) and Bed Bath &
Beyond (15) (1932 Broadway at W.
65th St., 917-441-9391, www.bed
bathandbeyond.com). There's also a
branch of Tower Records (16) (1961
Broadway, W. 66th/W. 67th Sts, 212-

799-2500, www.towerrecords.com), which is especially
renowned for its in-store performances by big names
such as Mariah Carey, Will Smith, and Ricky Martin.
Check its Web site for details. If the great outdoors is
your thing, Eastern Mountain Sports (17) (20 W. 61st St.
at Broadway, 212-397-4860, www.ems.com) has everything from backpacks to bicycles.

WHERE TO STAY

The area immediately around Lincoln Center is expensive, and you might want to consider moving a few
blocks uptown to some of the Upper West Side's less
expensive hotels (see page 147). But if you do want to
stay right by all the cultural action there's the Mandarin
Oriental New York (18) ($$$) (80 Columbus Circle at W.
60th St., 212-805-8800, www.mandarinoriental.com),
part of the Time Warner complex; it offers amazing park
views and prices to match. Or try the Trump International
Hotel & Tower (5) ($$$) (1 Central Park West at Columbus
Circle, 212-299-1001), which will lighten your wallet
even more.

UPPER WEST SIDE

B C to 72nd St., 81st St., 86th St., 96th St., 103rd St., Cathedral Parkway-110th St.; **1** to 79th St., 86th St., 96th St., 103rd St.; **2 3** to 72nd St., 96th St.

SNAPSHOT

The Upper West Side is the traditional liberal and intellectual heart of Manhattan, home to prominent museums and a wealthy, sophisticated populace. There's an endless and ongoing rivalry with the Upper East Side's denizens across the park, who are perceived by some to be more conservative, though the staggering escalation of real estate values and development in the West Side during the past few years has done much to blur this traditional boundary. It's *Seinfeld* territory, of course, and if Midtown is the iconic center of Manhattan with its skyscrapers, then the Upper West Side is the "regular guy" residential center of Manhattan for all those who aren't downtown-chic or Upper East Side-loaded: single or married with kids, this is where you come to live what passes for the "normal" life in Manhattan. As a result, it's a great place to explore for its vast array of restaurants, wonderful human-scaled side streets, and, of course, easy access to New York's great gem, Central Park, the development that brought the Upper West Side into being as a residential neighborhood in the first place during the late 19th century.

PLACES TO SEE
Landmarks:

The **Ansonia Hotel (20)** *(2109 Broadway, W. 73rd/W. 74th Sts., www.ansoniacondo.com)* is an amazing Beaux Arts building that is actually an apartment building, not a hotel. Its developer was a stickler for quality construction, including soundproof partitions, which resulted in numerous musicians living there, including Caruso and Stravinsky. Later it helped drown out the cries from Plato's Retreat, a notorious 1970s swinger club located there. **Central Park West (21)**, one of New York's most desirable addresses, runs up the west side of Central Park and is home to some of the finest residential buildings in the city. **The Dakota (22)** *(1 W. 72nd St. at Central Park West)* is probably the most famous of them, former home to John Lennon and current home of his widow, Yoko Ono. Hard to imagine it was once one of the sole buildings in a remote neighborhood when completed in 1884—hence its joking name, which stuck. If you look at Central Park West from Central Park, the Italian Renaissance-style twin towers of the **San Remo Apartments (23)** *(145-146 Central Park West, W. 74th/75th Sts.)* are among the most iconic. Bono just bought a little pad in one of them for around $15 million, joining a nest of other celebs there—a tough thing to do, considering Madonna was turned down by its co-op board. There are numerous religious and cultural institutions along Central Park West, and one of the handsomest is **Congregation Shearith Israel (24)** *(8 W. 70th St., www.shearith-israel.org)* a synagogue masquerading as a Georgian-style porticoed temple, built at

the turn of the 19th century. The lovely brownstone residential blocks between the park and the Hudson River are well worth exploring. Pick a random route and you'll come across all sorts of unexpected architectural treats. One of the loveliest is **Pomander Walk (25)** *(W. 94th/W. 95th Sts., Broadway/West End Aves.)*, an English-style mews of cottages running only one block and which creates a delightful mini-village atmosphere. **Riverside Drive (26)** *(W. 72nd St. to Fort Tryon Park)* is the other great residential address on the West Side, a majestic sweep that runs along the Hudson River and can best be appreciated from the water *(see Circle Line Cruises in "Times Square" on page 106)*. It's home to a combination of the old-moneyed intelligentsia and, increasingly, celebrities. Much of its charm derives from **Riverside Park (27)** *(W. 72nd St. to W. 153rd St., www.riversideparkfund.org)*, which runs next to it along the river, and is a brilliantly landscaped creation of Frederick Law Olmsted, co-creator of Central Park. Make note to see the **West 79th Street Marina and Boat Basin (28)** *(Hudson River at W. 79th St.)*, where a number of hardy souls, including entire families with children, live year round on houseboats. There's also an excellent cafe there *(see "Where to Eat," on page 144)*.

Arts & Entertainment:

The "big daddy" of museums here is the **American Museum of Natural History (31)** *(main entrance Central Park West at W. 79th St., 212-769-5400, www.amnh.*

org), which stretches alongside Central Park between W. 77th and W. 81st Streets. There are endless models and skeletons of dinosaurs, reptiles, and fish, as well as changing exhibits, an IMAX theater, and countless buttons to push. A relatively recent addition is the **Rose Center for Earth and Space (31)**, a Planetarium in an astounding glass box that will whisk you away on virtual reality tours to Mars and beyond. It's not to be missed. If you love live music, the Upper West Side is home to the **Beacon Theatre (32)** *(2124 Broadway, W. 74th/W. 75th Sts., 212-496-7070)* a mid-sized venue originally built in 1928 as a vaudeville palace that plays host to lesser-known acts and huge acts like the Stones and Bob Dylan when they want to play in more intimate venues. **Symphony Space (33)** *(2537 Broadway at W. 95th St., 212-864-5400, www.symphonyspace.org)* offers offbeat performance art of all kinds, including an excellent film, dance, literature, and film series, plus family theater events. At **El Taller Latino Americano (34)** *("The Latin American Workshop") (2710 Broadway at W. 104th St., 212-665-9460, www.tallerlatino.org)* you'll find classes and workshops from flamenco dancing to guitar playing, as well as frequent visits by Latino arts organizations.

Kids:

The **Children's Museum of Manhattan (36)** *(212 W. 83rd St., Broadway/Amsterdam Aves., 212-721-1223, www. cmom.org)* is a terrific resource for kids, offering play areas, drawing and music classes, workshops, interactive exhibits, and more. **Penny Whistle Toys (37)** *(448 Columbus Ave., W. 81st/W. 82nd Sts., 212-873-9090)* has a charming, if somewhat limited, choice of toys for children.

PLACES TO EAT & DRINK
Where to Eat:

Café Lalo (38) ($) *(201 W. 83rd St., Amsterdam Ave./ Broadway, 212-496-6031)* is brightly lit and crowded, but good for coffee and desserts. If you're an Anglophile, **Alice's Tea Cup (39) ($)** *(102 W. 73rd St., Amsterdam/ Columbus Aves., 212-799-3006, www.alicesteacup.com)* is the perfect place, with its cozy atmosphere and 200 blends of tea. The **Boat Basin Café (40) ($$)** *(W. 79th St. at the Hudson River, 212-496-5542, www.boatbasin cafe.com)* has great views and some of the best and most friendly barbecues in the city. **Café Luxembourg (41) ($$$)** *(200 W. 70th St., Amsterdam/Columbus Aves., 212-873-7411)* is a neighborhood classic. Great bistro food, very

stylish, and always crowded. Love hot dogs and a bargain? **Gray's Papaya (42) ($)** *(2090 Broadway at W. 72nd St., 212-799-0242)* can't be beat for its delicious dogs and cool fruit drinks. Heading uptown a bit, **Assaggio (43) ($$)** *(473*

Columbus Ave., W. 82nd/W. 83rd Sts., 212-877-0170) offers good basic Italian food, with sidewalk tables in the summer. At **Jean-Luc (44) ($$$)** *(507 Columbus Ave., W. 84th/W. 85th Sts., 212-712-1700, www.jeanlucrestaurant. com)* you'll find a lively young crowd chomping down on great French food with a view of Riverside Church. Long-time favorite **Carmine's (45) ($$)** *(2450 Broadway, W. 90th/W. 91st Sts., 212-362-2200, www.carmines nyc.com)* is for really pigging out on huge portions of basic Italian; best for groups and family outings. For seafood palates there's **Sipan (46) ($$)** *(702 Amsterdam Ave. at W. 94th St., 212-665-9929)*, a Peruvian restaurant that also has great drinks.

Bars & Nightlife:

Compass (48) *(208 W. 70th St., Amsterdam/West End Aves., 212-875-8600)*, a French-American bar and restaurant, brings a generally absent minimalist chic to this neck of the woods. Founded by soul duo Ashford & Simpson, **Sugar Bar (49)** *(254 W. 72nd St., Broadway/ West End Ave., 212-579-0222)* is a great African-themed bar with live soul and jazz and a reasonable cover. It also does a gospel brunch on Sundays. **Ruby Foo's (50)** *(2182 Broadway at W. 77th St., 212-724-6700, www.brguestrestaurants.com)* has excess written all over it and that's its charm: think glam, think Chinese, think cocktails. **Nice Matin (51)** *(201 W. 79th St. at Amsterdam Ave., 212-873-6423)* has a bizarre decorative scheme of warring colors and patterns, but the wide range of beers and wines by the glass will make you forget all that. The **Abbey Pub (60)** *(237 W. 105th, near* corner of Broadway, 212-222-8713) is the place for you if you take your drinking seriously. Beers, burgers, and three TV screens for watching sports make it a favorite local spot. Beware the more exotic fare on the menu.

WHERE TO SHOP

You can't say you've been to the Upper West Side till you've been to Zabar's (52) (2245 Broadway at W. 80th St., 212-787-2000, www.zabars.com), a food-cum-household appliance store that has amazing prices and great quality. Avoid coming on the weekend at all costs. H & H Bagels (53) (2239 Broadway at W. 80th St., 212-595-8003, www.hhbagels.com) was founded in 1972 and is the most famous bagel maker in the world, helped along by mentions on *Friends* and *Seinfeld*. It's open 24 hours. For a trifecta of food shopping classics, check out Barney Greengrass (54) (541 Amsterdam Ave., W. 86th/W. 87th Sts., 212-724-4707, www.barneygreengrass.com) with its pricey but fabulous sturgeon, lox, bialys, and more. For clothes try Barneys Co-Op (55) (2151 Broadway at W. 75th St., 646-335-0978, www.barneys. com) a hipper, edgier spinoff of the main Barneys store on Madison Avenue. (See the Upper East Side's "Where to Shop," on page 159.) For women's clothes there's the

ever-playful Betsey Johnson (56) (248 Columbus Ave., W. 71st/W. 72nd Sts., 212-362-3364, www.betseyjohnson. com) for fun, flirty dresses and the like. Robert Marc (57) (190 Columbus Ave., W. 68th/W. 69th Sts., 212-799-4600, *www.robertmarc.com)* has several stores around town offering some seriously cool spectacles. Finally, just want to look without (probably) buying? Maxilla & Mandible (58) *(451 Columbus Ave., W. 81st/W. 82nd Sts., 212-724-6173, www.maxillaandmandible.com)* is where the young Indiana Jones in the making goes for his animal and fish skeletons. Bizarre but fun.

WHERE TO STAY

The Amsterdam Inn (59) ($) *(340 Amsterdam Ave. at W. 76th St., 212-579-7500)* offers 30 rooms, with both shared and private baths, all at reasonable rates. On the Ave Hotel (19) ($$) *(2178 Broadway at W. 77th St., 212-362-1100, www.ontheave-nyc.com)* is a mid-priced hotel with great views of Central Park and more style than many hotels in this neighborhood.

chapter 7

UPPER EAST SIDE

CENTRAL PARK

UPPER EAST SIDE
CENTRAL PARK

Places to See:

1. 11 East 62nd Street
2. 11 East 73rd Street
3. 45 East 66th Street Apartments
4. Carl Schurz Park
5. Gracie Mansion
6. Carnegie Hill
7. Yorkville
8. Jewish Museum
9. Solomon R. Guggenheim Museum
10. Cooper-Hewitt National Design Museum
11. Rhinelander Mansion
12. Metropolitan Museum of Art
13. Loeb Boathouse/ Central Park Boathouse Restaurant
14. Bow Bridge
15. Whitney Museum of American Art
16. Frick Collection
17. Asia Society and Museum
48. The Pond
49. Wollman Rink
50. The Dairy
51. Central Park Zoo
52. Heckscher Playground
53. Sheep Meadow
54. Strawberry Fields
55. The Lake
56. Bethesda Fountain and Terrace
57. The Ramble
58. Delacorte Theater
59. Belvedere Castle/ Henry Luce Nature Observatory
60. Tisch Children's Zoo
61. The Great Lawn
62. Jacqueline Kennedy Onassis Reservoir
63. North Meadow Recreation Center
64. Harlem Meer
65. Conservatory Garden
66. Charles A. Dana Discovery Center
67. The Carousel

Places to Eat & Drink:

18. Tavern on the Green
19. EJ's Luncheonette
21. Aureole
22. East
23. Jackson Hole
24. Due
25. Marks
26. Beyoglu
27. Elaine's
28. Heidelberg
29. Vico
30. Zebú Grill
31. Stir
32. Cipriani's
33. Club Macanudo
34. Bemelmans Bar
35. Brother Jimmy's Bait Shack
36. Iggy's Legendary
    Karaoke Bar

Where to Shop:

20. Jacadi
37. Hermès
38. Jimmy Choo
39. Barneys New York
40. Prada
41. Morgane Le Fay
42. Memorial Sloan-Kettering
    Cancer Center Thrift Shop
43. Pookie & Sebastian
44. Lyric Hi-Fi, Inc.

Where to Stay:

45. Carlyle Hotel
46. Hotel Wales
47. Gracie Inn

UPPER EAST SIDE

● SNAPSHOT ●

The Upper East Side is an astonishingly varied and rich
(in every sense of the word) part of the city. A brief stroll
around the ritzier stretches of Fifth or Madison avenues
will certainly reveal more than a fair share of frosty
blondes with Pekinese in tow or imperious old ladies
being helped out of taxis by obsequious doormen, but
it's much more than that. The stretches east of
Lexington Avenue ("The East Upper East Side") resem-
ble the Upper West Side in their relatively democratic
social make-up. There is also the cultural bounty of the
area to consider: "Museum Mile" with its amazing cluster of world-class museums, and some of the most
mouth-watering architecture in the city.

PLACES TO SEE
Landmarks:

The heart of chic and moneyed
New York is the so-called **"Gold**
Coast," which runs for about a
mile between E. 60th and E. 80th
streets from Fifth Avenue to Park
Avenue. This was the area where
the gilded-age robber barons built

their new park-side mansions when Central Park came into being. Many of these buildings have since been converted either to apartments or consulates. One of the most amazing is **11 E. 62nd Street (1)** *(Fifth/Madison Aves.)*, a former private mansion now home to Japan's UN representative. The opulence of its limestone façade and Beaux Arts details still amazes today in a world of Donald Trump high-rises. Another example is **11 E. 73rd St. (2)** *(Fifth/Madison Aves.)*, originally the Joseph and Kate Pulitzer House (of Pulitzer Prize renown), now converted into apartments. Around the turn of the 19th century the rich began to leave their beautiful, yet hard-to-keep-up, mansions and moved to the latest architectural invention—the apartment building. Naturally they sacrificed nothing in terms of style, as the **45 East 66th Street Apartments (3)** *(Madison/Park Aves.)* demonstrate. With its lovely Gothic details and large windows it's as desirable a residence today as it was nearly 100 years ago. With an average per-resident income of around $200,000 a year (south of E. 96th Street, that is), Park Avenue deserves its wealthy reputation. Yet its secret is that it is actually built over railroad tracks that had been an open trench and eyesore for many years until they were covered over around the turn of the century. At E. 96th Street, Park Avenue's little secret emerges from underground and the character of the street and the surrounding neighborhood changes drastically. It's fun to watch the trains come crawling out of the dark here. Along the waterfront there's **Carl Schurz Park (4)** *(East River between E. 84th/E. 90th Sts., www.carlschurzparknyc.org)*, a beautifully designed park built out ingeniously over the FDR Drive below. It affords amazing views across to Queens on the other side. The park contains the Mayor's official residence, **Gracie Mansion (5)** *(E. 88th St. at East End Ave., 212-570-4751)*, Manhattan's sole remaining Federal-style house, which is now open to the public, though you must reserve ahead of time for tours.

The designation "Upper East Side" incorporates several other residential areas that are worth exploring, including **Carnegie Hill (6)** *(E. 86th to E. 96th Sts., Fifth/Third Aves.)* and **Yorkville (7)** *(E. 72th to E. 96th Sts., Central Park/East River)*. Both are filled with elegant tree-lined streets and fine shops and restaurants. Carnegie Hill in particular is home to a number of superb museums, including the **Jewish Museum (8)** *(1109 Fifth Ave. at E. 92nd St., 212-423-3200, www.thejewishmuseum.org)*; the **Solomon R. Guggenheim Museum (9)** *(1071 Fifth Ave. at E. 89th St., 212-360-3500, www.guggenheim.org)*; and the **Cooper-Hewitt National Design Museum (10)** *(2 E. 91st St. at Fifth Ave., 212-849-8400, www.ndm.si.edu)*, which was converted from steel magnate Andrew Carnegie's private 1902 mansion, and ignited development in this area at the time *(see "Arts & Entertainment," page 155)*. Yorkville became a notably German neighborhood, and the wealthy Rhinelander family in particular built many beautiful mansions and apartment buildings here in conjunction with architect Henry Hardenbergh, designer of the Dakota Building. The most famous of these is the **Rhinelander Mansion (11)** *(867 Madison Ave., E. 71st/E. 72nd Sts.)*, a stunning building, both inside and out, that's now home to Ralph Lauren's Polo empire in New York.

Arts & Entertainment:

The Upper East Side is high-brow heaven, with the greatest concentration of museums in the city. **"Museum Mile"** is the name given to the stretch of cultural institutions that runs along Fifth Avenue from E. 82nd to E. 104th Streets. The biggest and most famous of them all is the **Metropolitan Museum of Art (12)** *(1000 Fifth Ave. at E. 82nd St., 212-535-7710, www.metmuseum.org)*, a vast treasure house that runs four blocks north up Fifth Avenue and expands deeply into Central Park at the back. The Met's slogan is "5000 years of art," and they aren't kidding; walking into its vast central rotunda with galleries radiating off it can be intimidating. It's best to choose a particular part—European painting, Egyptian art—and enjoy it in detail rather than attempt the impossible and try to "see it all." On Fridays and Saturdays the Met hosts a string quartet and cocktails upstairs, which is expensive but one of the best people-watching events in the city—look out for all those nervous first daters. From classical temple to outrageous modern swirl, the **Solomon R. Guggenheim Museum (9)** *(1071 Fifth Ave. at E. 89th St., 212-423-3500, www. guggenheim. org)* couldn't be more

different from the Met. Its circular concrete structure that seems to twist itself out of the ground is architect Frank Lloyd Wright's most iconic structure. Inside, this spiral is even more amazing, though opinion is divided about how successful a space it is to actually view the modern art on exhibit there. Further north is the **Cooper-Hewitt National Design Museum (10)** *(2 E. 91st St. at Fifth Ave., 212-849-8400, www.cooperhewitt.org),* a handsome limestone-clad building that's dedicated to the history of design, both domestic and industrial. Expect to find exhibitions covering eclectic subject matter from wallpaper to silverware to classic 1960s road maps, to name but a few recent ones. The **Jewish Museum (8)** *(1109 Fifth Ave. at E. 92nd St., 212-423-3200, www.thejewishmuseum.org)* is housed in a 1908 chateau and has a large permanent collection of artifacts related to Jewish life and culture, in addition to hosting impressive temporary exhibitions. There's also a kosher cafe. Off Museum Mile are a few other major museums, including the **Whitney Museum of American Art (15)** *(945 Madison Ave. at E. 75th St., 212-570-3676, www.whitney. org).* Its fortress-like façade puts many off, but inside there's a plethora of amazing art, by such artists as Edward Hopper, Willem de Kooning, and Georgia O'Keeffe. Far more sedate is the **Frick Collection (16)** *(1 E. 70th St., Fifth/Madison Aves., 212-288-0700, www. frick.org),* a charming classical mansion once owned by industrialist Henry Clay Frick. It has a garden surrounding it, an indoor pool, and a terrific collection of old masters, including Vermeer, Van Dyke, and Rembrandt. Finally, there's the **Asia Society and Museum (17)** *(725 Park Ave. at E. 70th St., 212-288-6400, www.asiasociety. org),* housed in a sleek modern building with a spacious interior that does justice to the delicacy of the works on display. There's an Asian restaurant attached where the food is artfully prepared and just as pleasing to the taste buds.

Kids:

The main attraction for kids here is **Central Park** and its numerous activities *(see "Central Park, Kids" on pages 166-167)*, but **Carl Schurz Park (4)** *(East River between E. 84th/E. 90th Sts.)* is also wonderful for children, in particular the playground at E. 84th Street and East End Avenue. **EJ's Luncheonette (19)** *(1271 Third Ave. at E. 73rd St., 212-472-0600)* is loud, kid-friendly, and cheap. Jacadi **(20)** *(1296 Madison Ave. at E. 92nd St., 212-369-1616, www.jacadiusa.com)* offers French clothes if you want to make your baseball-cap-wearing little darling look more Euro. There are several other branches in the Upper East Side as well.

PLACES TO EAT & DRINK
Where to Eat:

The Upper East Side doesn't boast the array of top-class restaurants that Downtown does. With some notable exceptions, the area is full of "local favorites"—good but not overly exciting. One of those exceptions is **Aureole (21) ($$$)** *(34 E. 61st St., Madison/Park Aves., 212-319-1660, www.charliepalmer.com)*, where the new American food is outstanding, and comes served in an elegant

town house. If you like sushi but don't like being gouged, try the mini chain **East (22) ($$)** *(354 E. 66th St., First/Second Aves., 212-734-5270)*. For good burgers and other American fare there's **Jackson Hole (23) ($$)** *(232 E. 64th St, Second/Third Aves., 212-371-7187, www.jacksonholeburgers.com)*. In the 70s there's **Due (24) ($$)** *(1396 Third Ave., E. 79th/E. 80th Sts., 212-772-3331, cash only)* for good Northern Italian, or for something fancier **Marks (25) ($$$)** *(The Mark Hotel, 25 E. 77th St., Fifth/Madison Aves., 212-879-1864)*, which offers great food and a large wine list in a romantic, muted atmosphere. In the 80s there's **Beyoglu (26) ($$)** *(1431 Third Ave. at E. 81st St., 212-650-0850)*, an excellent  Mediterranean-Turkish place where the best thing to do is share a bunch of the fresh appetizers. If you fancy some star-spotting with your Italian-American food try **Elaine's (27) ($$$)** *(1703 Second Ave., E. 88th/E. 89th Sts., 212-534-8103)*. A remnant of the old German community in Yorkville is **Heidelberg (28) ($$)** *(1648 Second Ave., E. 85th/E. 86th Sts., 212-628-2332, www.heidelbergrestaurant.com)*, which has kitschy décor but solid portions. In the 90s, try **Vico (29) ($$$)** *(1302 Madison Ave., E. 92nd/E. 93rd Sts., 212-876-2222, cash only)* if you want to splurge on really good Italian food. An unusual Brazilian outpost up here is **Zebú Grill (30) ($$)** *(305 E. 92nd St., First/Second Aves., 212-426-7500)*, which offers a really lively vibe, especially for this neighborhood, and truly flavorful food.

Bars & Nightlife:

Stir (31) *(1363 First Ave. at E. 73rd St., 212-744-7190)* is an exposed-brick minimalist bar that claims to "bring the flavor of Downtown to the Upper East Side." Far more old-school is **Cipriani's (32)** *(781 Fifth Ave., E. 59th/E. 60th Sts., 212-753-5566, www.cipriani.com)*, where waiters in tuxes create a potentially daunting atmosphere for some, though it's a true New York experience. **Club Macanudo (33)** *(26 E. 63rd St., Park/Madison Aves., 212-752-8200, www.clubmacanudo.com)* is for those who like to smoke cigars (Yes! You can still smoke here.) while swilling a single malt. It's pricey and you need to dress up. **Bemelmans Bar (34)** *(Carlyle Hotel, 35 E. 76th St. at Madison Ave., 212-744-1600, www.the carlyle.com)* is classic New York—a gentleman's club ambience with plush chairs, cozy décor, steep drinks, and wonderful live jazz. If all this is a bit too mature for your taste, there's another, more youthful, aspect to the Upper East Side's bar and club scene, as represented by **Brother Jimmy's Bait Shack (35)** *(1644 Third Ave., at E. 92nd St., 212-426-2020, www.brotherjimmys.com)*, a frat-boy paradise with beer and barbecues. Be warned. In a similar vein there's also **Iggy's Legendary Karaoke Bar (36)** *(1452 Second Ave., E. 75th/E. 76th Sts., 212-327-3043)*, where a lethal combo of cheap beers and even cheaper music can be had every night.

WHERE TO SHOP

The Upper East Side's prime shopping strip is Madison Avenue, where all the famous designers have their flagship stores. Parisian-style merchant Hermès (37) *(691 Madison Ave. at E. 62nd St., 212-751-3181, www. hermes.com)* offers its famous scarves and much more at this spacious store. If you're a foot fetishist, then Jimmy

Choo (38) *(716 Madison Ave., E. 63rd/E. 64th Sts., 212-759-7078, www.jimmychoo.com)* is your Nirvana. You can find sexy high-heeled creations that will make you feel part of the *Sex and the City* cast. Barneys New York (39) *(660 Madison Ave. at E. 61st St., 212-826-8900, www.barneys.com)* has classic menswear and women's clothes too, as well as a beauty store, a super-cool restaurant, and price tags that read like fiction. Prada (40) *(841 Madison Ave. at E. 70th St., 212-327-4200, www.prada.com)* sells a whole range of men and women's wear, but it's those shoes with the little red tag on the heel that really count. Morgane Le Fay (41) *(746 Madison Ave., E. 64th/E. 65th Sts., 212-879-9700, www.morganelefay.com)* offers beautifully bizarre, almost architectural, gowns and dresses at suitably architectural prices. Less expensive stores can be found east of Lexington Avenue. Ratcheting down the prices considerably is the Memorial Sloan-Kettering Cancer Center Thrift Shop (42) *(1440 Third Ave., E. 81st/E. 82nd Sts., 212-535-1250)*, which has some real bargains, as the ladies who lunch often drop off their unwanted couture here. This is one of the best thrift shops in the city. At Pookie & Sebastian (43) *(1488 Second Ave., E. 77th/E. 78th Sts., 212-861-0550)* you can get cutting-edge fashion, including a whole array of designer jeans, at much reduced prices. Finally, if you're a hi-fi nut, Lyric Hi-Fi, Inc. (44) *(1221 Lexington Ave., E. 82nd/E. 83rd Sts., 212-439-1900, www.lyricusa.com)* has great offers on a wide range of stuff, and a knowledgeable staff.

WHERE TO STAY

If money's no object you can't beat the venerable Carlyle Hotel (45) ($$$) *(35 E. 76th St., Madison/Park Aves., 212-744-1600, www.thecarlyle.com)*. It has **Bemelmans Bar (34)** *(see "Bars & Nightlife," on page 158),* famous for its animal murals by Ludwig Bemelmans, the creator of the *Madeleine* books, who was a former resident of the hotel. After 9:30 PM there's live music with a steep cover, but it's worth it. The 100-year-old Hotel Wales (46) ($$) *(1295 Madison Ave. at E. 92nd St., 212-876-6000, www.waleshotel.com)* is a lovely hotel that feels like you're entering a private (albeit grand) house. It's also very child-friendly. For a budget there's the Gracie Inn (47) ($) *(502 E. 81st St., York/East End Aves., 212-628-1700),* tucked away in a town house far from the subway but well worth it for the low, low prices.

To East Side of the Park:

4 5 to 59th St. or 86th St.; 6 to 59th St., 68th St., 77th St., 86th St., 96th St., 103rd St., 110th St.

To West Side of the Park:

B C to 59th St.-Columbus Circle, 72nd St., 81st St., 86th St., 96th St., 103rd St., 110th St.-Cathedral Parkway; A to 59th St.-Columbus Circle

To Southern Side of the Park:

B D E to Seventh Ave.;
N Q R W to 57th St.-Seventh Ave.;
F to 57th St.; N R W to Fifth Ave.-59th St.

To Northern Side of the Park:

2 3 to Central Park North-110th St.

● SNAPSHOT ●

It's impossible to conceive of New York without Central Park, yet for years the city existed without any major public park for its teeming citizens. Old photographs and engravings reveal a rocky expanse complete with wooden shacks, grazing goats, swamps, and encampments of the city's dispossessed. In the mid-19th century, the city's elders were finally piqued by their great rivals in London and Paris to do something about this, and commissioned landscape designer Frederick

Law Olmsted and architect Calvert Vaux to convert a vast chunk of this unruly land into a picturesque European-style park worthy of a great city. This of course they did (along with several other parks in New York), and the results were astonishing. Not only did New York gain an enormous and beautiful green space, but the effect was also to galvanize development around the park, turning what even in the 1880s was still a largely undeveloped rural suburb of the city into a social and architectural center every bit the equal of its European counterparts.

PLACES TO SEE
Landmarks:

Southern Section (Central Park South to 72nd Street):
Olmsted and Vaux adopted the three principal elements of 18th-century British Picturesque design—water, landscaping, and architecture—to create their masterpiece, and these elements have only improved with time. Enter Central Park from the southeast and you'll encounter **The Pond (48)** *(approx. Fifth/Sixth Aves. between 60th/62nd Sts.)*—an artfully placed body of water with ducks and swans floating on it. Turn around and gaze south over The Pond at the skyline of Central

Park South rising above it for one of the most knockout views in the city. Just north of The Pond is the **Wollman Rink (49)** *(just north of the park entrance at Sixth Ave./Central Park South, www.wollmanskatingrink.com, see also "Kids," on page 166)*—a rival to the Rink at Rockefeller Center for the most romantic spot in the city. Built in the 1950s, it fell into disrepair and the city claimed it was unable to restore it. Enter Donald Trump on a

white horse, who not only repaired it ahead of schedule, but did so $750,000 under budget. Naturally, it's now emblazoned with his name. Just north of the rink is **The Dairy (50)** *(mid-park at 65th St.)*, Vaux's delightful Victorian Gothic confection. It used to be a real working dairy, but now operates as an information center for the park, and organized tours depart here (212-794-6564 for details). The other major landmarks in this southern section of the park are the **Central Park Zoo (51)** *(830 Fifth Ave., E. 63rd/E. 66th Sts., 212-439-6500, www.centralparkzoo.org)* and the **Heckscher Playground (52)** *(Seventh Ave., W. 61st/W. 63rd Sts.)*. *(See "Kids," on page 166 for details of both.)* The biggest open space in the southern section of the park is the **Sheep Meadow (53)** *(starts at 66th St.)*, a designated quiet zone where sheep used to graze until as late as 1934. Nearby is **Strawberry Fields (54)** *(W. 72nd St at Central Park West)*, a former favorite spot of John Lennon, who lived in the Dakota Apartments across from the park. If you're a Beatles fan it may be a must, if not, be warned: it's often full of sappy guitar-twanging mourners paying "tribute."

Mid-park (72nd through 79th Sts.):

North and slightly east is **The Lake (55)**, with its beautiful **Loeb Boathouse (13)** *(mid-park at 75th St.)* and

163

charming **Bow Bridge (14)**. You can rent boats and even a gondola here. Near the lake is the lovely **Bethesda Fountain and Terrace (56)** *(mid-park, by the 72nd St. Transverse Road)*, which is one of the social hives of the park, full of every type of character on earth on a hot summer's day. **The Ramble (57)** *(mid-park from 72nd through 79th Sts.)*, where pathways twist amongst brush and trees, is east of the Lake, and one of the best places for bird watching. Just north of the Ramble are two architectural landmarks, the **Delacorte Theater (58)** *(mid-park at 80th St., see "Arts & Entertainment," on page 166)* and **Belvedere Castle (59)** *(mid-park at 79th St.)*—a Victorian stone block fantasy that rises majestically to the highest point in the park, offering superb views. It's also the location of the **Henry Luce Nature Observatory (59)** *(see "Arts & Entertainment," on page 165)*. As you move north over the 79th Street Transverse Road you come across a sweeping open expanse—**The Great Lawn (61)** *(mid-park, 79th/86th Sts.)*. A reservoir until the 1930s, it then became the place for New Yorkers to fool around—socializing, flirting, playing games, or just

plain soaking up the sun. During the summer the Met and the Philharmonic stage free operas and concerts here *(see "Arts & Entertainment," page 166)*, and the Lawn has played host to huge shows by the likes of Simon and Garfunkel and Garth Brooks. A reservoir still exists north of the 86th Street Transverse Road, now renamed **Jacqueline Kennedy Onassis Reservoir**

(62) *(mid-park, 85th/96th Sts.)*. She was one of the thousands of people who used the popular jogging path around it, which is still in use.

North Section (97th through 110th Sts.):

North of the 97th Street Transverse Road at mid-park is the **North Meadow Recreation Center (63)** *(see "Arts & Entertainment," on page 166)*, a handsomely restored recreation facility set amidst the 23 acres of the North Meadow. The northernmost reaches of the park are some of the most beautiful and contrasting, with the wild beauty of the 11-acre **Harlem Meer (64)** *(NE corner of the park, 106th/109th Sts.)*, a lake where you can fish from mid-April through mid-October, and the formal landscaping of the **Conservatory Garden (65)** *(Fifth Ave. at E. 105th St., 212-360-2766)*.

Arts & Entertainment:

In Central Park it's hard to distinguish between kids' and adults' entertainment, so check out "Kids" on page 166 as well. For information on all activities, prices, and admission times, visit www.centralpark.org. If you're into fishing (strictly catch-and-release), the **Charles A. Dana Discovery Center (66)** *(Malcolm X Blvd. at 110th St., 212-860-1370)* will rent you equipment for fishing in nearby Harlem Meer. You can also meet up for bird-watching tours here, as well as take part in various family and children's workshops. Bird-watching and history tours also depart from the **Henry Luce Nature Observatory (59)** *(see "Landmarks," page 164)*, which has microscopes, exhibits, and interactive displays for children, too. The **North Meadow Recreation Center (63)** *(mid-park at 97th St., 212-348-4867)* was converted from stables to a recreation center in the 1990s, and offers soccer, softball and 12 baseball fields for school and public use. Balls, bats, and other equipment can be rented inexpensively. For culture lovers, there are the **summer outdoor music shows** *(see www.summerstage.org or www.centralparknyc.org for details)*, with everything from classical concerts by the New York Philharmonic to free rock concerts. Every summer the **Delacorte Theater (58)** *(mid-park at 80th St., www.public theater.org)* presents its free annual Shakespeare in the Park Festival, featuring big name talent (e.g., Jimmy Smits, Patrick Stewart). There's also a host of other activities you can do, from chess to biking to blading. (Equipment for all three can be rented in the park.)

Kids:

The **Heckscher Playground (52)** *(Seventh Ave., 61st/63rd Sts.)* is the biggest playground in Central Park (three acres), filled with swings and other amusements, plus excellent bathrooms. **The Carousel (67)** *(mid-park at 65th St., 212-879-0244 for info)* offers rides on beautiful hand-painted wooden horses for a dollar; it's an attraction that's been going since 1871. The **Wollman Rink (49)** *(just north of the park entrance at Sixth Ave./59th St., www.wollmanskatingrink.com, 212-439-6900)* is a year-round attraction for children and adults alike. In the winter you can arrange for children's special skating classes with qualified teachers, and in the summer the rink is transformed into a delightful family center with a mini-carousel, rides, face-painting, games, cotton candy, and all kinds of other attractions. The **Central Park Zoo (51)** *(830 Fifth Ave., 63rd/66th Sts., 212-439-6500, www.centralparkzoo.org)*, of course, is the biggest children's attraction, and there are actually two of them—the **Tisch Children's Zoo (60)**, which is essentially a petting zoo with goats, sheep, and other domestic animals, and the main zoo itself, home to polar bears, sea lions, penguins, and much more, all painstakingly arranged in simulations of their natural habitats. If you can afford it, there are even overnight pajama parties for kids to learn about the animals. Avoid the lackluster food at the cafe.

PLACES TO EAT & DRINK
Where to Eat:

There's the classic hot dog and pretzel stands dotted around the park, or you can try the **Central Park Boathouse Restaurant (13) ($$$)** *(see Loeb Boathouse in "Landmarks," on page 163)* *(mid-park at 75th St., 212-517-2233)*, though it's expensive and pretty limited. If you don't mind spending money and want a real New York experience, there's **Tavern on the Green (18) ($$$)** *(off Central Park West at 67th St., 212-873-3200, www.tavernonthegreen.com)*, built in 1870 for the sheep that grazed in Sheep Meadow, before being converted into a restaurant and bar in 1934. The Tavern hosts great live music, especially jazz and cabaret, offers dazzling views, and is lit up like a jewel at night—though all this will set you back a packet, naturally.

chapter 8

HARLEM & SPANISH HARLEM

MORNINGSIDE HEIGHTS

WASHINGTON HEIGHTS & INWOOD

HARLEM & SPANISH HARLEM MORNINGSIDE HEIGHTS WASHINGTON HEIGHTS & INWOOD

Places to See:

1. Apollo Theater
2. Strivers' Row
3. Hamilton Heights Historic District
4. Abyssinian Baptist Church
5. Mount Morris Park
6. Trinity Cemetery
7. Graffiti Hall of Fame
8. Schomburg Center for Research in Black Culture
9. Studio Museum in Harlem
10. National Black Theater
11. Museo del Barrio
30. Cathedral Church of St. John the Divine
31. Columbia University
32. Low Memorial Library
33. Morningside Park
41. George Washington Bridge
42. Fort Tryon Park
43. Cloisters Museum/Cloisters Gift Shop
44. Inwood Hill Park
45. Henry Hudson Bridge
46. Morris-Jumel Mansion
53. Riverside Church
54. Grant's Tomb
55. Museum of the City of New York

Places to Eat & Drink:

12. Amy Ruth's
13. Bayou
14. Londel's Supper Club
15. Revival
16. Carlito's Café
17. La Hacienda
18. Platto d'Oro
19. Cotton Club
20. Lenox Lounge
21. Showman's Bar
22. St. Nick's Pub
34. Kitchenette Uptown
35. Max Soha
36. Terrace in the Sky
37. Le Monde
38. Heights Bar and Grill
47. New Leaf Café
48. Bohio
49. DR-K
50. Viva

Sometimes I feel discriminated against,
but it does not make me angry.
It merely astonishes me.
How can anyone deny themselves
the pleasure of my company?

—*Zora Neale Hurston*

HARLEM & SPANISH HARLEM

HARLEM: **B** **C** *to 110th St.-Cathedral Parkway, 116th St., 125th St., 135th St., 145th St.;* **B** **D** *to 155th St.;* **2** **3** *to Central Park North-110th St., 116th St., 125th St., 135th St.;* **3** *to 145 St.;* **4** **5** **6** *to 125 St.*

SPANISH HARLEM: **6** *to 96th St., 103rd St., 110th St., 116th St., 125 St.;* **4** **5** *to 125th St.*

◆ SNAPSHOT ◆

Visitors to Manhattan often stop short north of Central Park, or at the most take a trip to the Cloisters museum at Manhattan's far northern tip, which is a shame, because the numerous and varied neighborhoods of this area are fascinating places to explore. Harlem *(110th St. to the Harlem River, Morningside/Saint Nicholas Aves.)*, the most famous, has been a center of African-American life in New York since the early years of the 20th century, and after a long period of turbulence in the 1960s and 1970s, is undergoing a major renaissance, with its historic buildings being restored by homesteaders (both black and white) and new capital injected into its stores and businesses. Spanish Harlem *(E. 96th St. to E. 120th Sts., approx., Fifth/Third Aves.)*, or El Barrio ("The Neighborhood"), as it's called by its largely Puerto Rican population, has yet to attract the influx of capital that Harlem has, but is still well worth visiting for its street life and delicious, inexpensive food.

PLACES TO SEE
Landmarks:

One of the most famous landmarks is the **Apollo Theater (1)** *(253 W. 125th St., Adam Clayton Powell Jr. Blvd./Frederick Douglass Blvd., 212-531-5305, www.apollotheater.com).* It was here that Michael Jackson, Ella Fitzgerald, and a host of other R&B and soul stars got their start. The TV program *Showtime at the Apollo* is broadcast from here every week; it's funny, enjoyable, and brutal if the audience doesn't like you. The venue also hosts major rock stars such as Van Morrison when they're looking for smaller places with old-time ambience. Harlem has some of the best 19th-century residential architecture in the country, now in a flurry of restoration in many places. Check out **Strivers' Row (2)** *(W. 138th to W. 139th Sts., Powell/Douglass Blvds.),* a block of beautiful Renaissance-style brick row houses, designed in part by McKim, Mead & White in 1890. As the area became increasingly African-American, the black middle classes moved into the block and the term "Strivers' Row" gained popular usage. The other major area for handsome row houses is in the **Hamilton Heights Historic District (3)** *(W. 140th/W. 145th Sts., Amsterdam/Edgecomb Aves.).* In particular, note the lovely houses on

Convent Avenue, near W. 148th Street, with their curving stoops and bay windows. The **Abyssinian Baptist Church (4)** *(132 Odell Clark Place, formerly West 138th St., Adam Clayton Powell, Jr./Malcolm X Blvds., also known as 7th and Lenox Aves., 212-862-7474, www.abyssinian.org)* is the most well-known of Harlem's numerous churches, and offers wonderful services with gospel singing. If you're interested in gospel tours of Harlem, many companies offer them, generally with brunch or drinks included. (Note that large groups are required to register with this and other churches in advance, especially on Sundays.) Harlem has several lovely parks and open spaces, and **Mount Morris Park (5)** *(W. 120th/W. 124th Sts., Madison Ave./Mount Morris Park West),* also known as Marcus Garvey Park, is the most historic. Only a few years ago many of the houses surrounding it were simply shells, or grimly hanging on as rooming houses, but the establishment of a Historic District and the recent frenzy of restoration, by whites, African-Americans, and Caribbeans alike, has restored these buildings to their original splendor. **Trinity Cemetery (6)** *(W. 153rd/W. 155th Sts., Riverside Drive/ Amsterdam Ave.)* has some of the oldest graves in the city (including those of notable New Yorkers John James Audubon and John Jacob Astor), with great views over the Hudson River. In Spanish Harlem, check out the **Graffiti Hall of Fame (7)** *(W. 106th St., Madison/Park Aves.),* where the long walls are covered in brilliantly colored images by masters, old-school and otherwise. **Riverside Church (53)** *(490 Riverside Drive at W. 120th St., www.theriversidechurchny.org)* is one of the city's

173

great landmarks, a Rockefeller-funded project that rises 21 stories and has a not-to-be-missed observation deck in its bell tower. **Grant's Tomb (54)** *(Riverside Drive at W. 122nd St., www.nps.gov/gegr),* formerly known as the General Grant National Memorial, was the city's number one tourist attraction in the early years of the 20th century. Its attraction has waned, but this domed classical monument is still worth a visit and is open daily.

Arts & Entertainment:

As befits a neighborhood so rich in cultural history—with figures such as writers Zora Neale Hurston and Langston Hughes, and musicians Fats Waller, Duke Ellington, and Louis Armstrong; all lived or worked there in the 1920s and 1930s—Harlem has a large number of first-class cultural institutions. Its musical heritage is kept alive in its clubs and bars *(see "Bars & Nightlife," pages 176-177),* but for a general cultural record of black America the **Schomburg Center for Research in Black Culture (8)** *(515 Malcolm X Blvd. at W. 135th St., 212-491-2200, www.nypl.org/research/sc/sc. html)* can't be beat. The center offers a permanent collection of documents, books, films, and more, and excellent exhibitions—a genuinely moving and informative experience that can be appreciated by all, no matter what your ethnicity. The **Studio Museum in Harlem (9)** *(144 W. 125th St., Malcolm X/Adam Clayton Powell Jr. Blvds., 212-864-4500, www.studiomuseum.org, cash only)* was founded in 1968 as a space in which to exhibit work by black artists, both American and foreign. It offers such programming as lecture series, artists in residence, and extremely varied exhibitions from painters and sculptors to African comic artists. The **National Black Theater (10)** *(2031 Fifth Ave., W. 125th/W. 126th Sts., 212-722-3800, www. nationalblacktheater.org)* is an enormous 64,000 square-foot building that's broken up inside into a number of much smaller, more intimate performing areas, decorated with African art and décor. Plays and other forms of performances here emphasize black culture and history. Spanish Harlem has its own equivalent to the Studio Museum in Harlem, the **Museo del Barrio (11)** *(1230 Fifth Ave., E. 104th/E. 105th Sts., 212-831-7272, www. elmuseo.org)*. It has a large and varied collection of works by Latino artists, both living abroad and resident in the U.S., as well as excellent temporary exhibits. The **Museum of the City of New York (55)** *(1220 Fifth Ave., E. 103rd/E. 104th Sts., 212-534-1672, www.mcny.org)* houses a delightful collection of artifacts that reveal the history of the city from colonial times to the present, including photographs, paintings, and documents. There's also a touching collection of more personal effects such as children's toys, diaries, and other ephemera.

PLACES TO EAT & DRINK
Where to Eat:
Don't come to Harlem expecting to eat light: soul food is the name of the game here, and it's the best in the city. At **Amy Ruth's (12) ($)** *(113 W. 116th St., Lenox/Seventh Aves., 212-280-8779, www.amyruthsrestaurant.com)* you'll get stuffed for a very reasonable cost in an extremely friendly atmosphere. **Bayou (13) ($$)** *(308*

Malcolm X Blvd., W. 125th/W. 126th Sts., 212-426-3800) is a little more expensive, but its Cajun-Creole food is delicious and they do a great Sunday brunch. **Londel's Supper Club (14) ($$)** *(2620 Frederick Douglass Blvd., W. 139th/W. 140th Sts., 212-234-6114)* also does a sterling Sunday brunch and has some of the best soul food in town. If you're looking for a more romantic spot to go before or after a jazz show, check out **Revival (15) ($$)** *(2367 Frederick Douglass Blvd. at W. 127th St., 212-222-8338),* which offers a darkened atmosphere in which to enjoy its excellent French-Caribbean food. In Spanish Harlem, visit the tiny but wonderful **Carlito's Café (16) ($)** *(1701 Lexington Ave. at E. 106th St., 212-348-7044),* which serves not just as a place to get a tasty bite but as a performing arts space for everyone from rappers to Latin American guitarists to belly dancers. **La Hacienda (17) ($)** *(219 E. 116th St., Second/Third Aves., 212-987-1617)* will re-awaken your palate with Mexican-with-a-twist food such as grilled steak with cactus and terrific (and cheap) papaya and mango drinks. At **Platto d'Oro (18) ($$)** *(34 E. 109th St. at First Ave., 212-828-2929)* you'll find inventive and delicious risottos and fish dishes in large portions.

Bars & Nightlife:

Harlem is hopping with nightlife, and with crime both in Harlem and citywide at an all-time low, don't be afraid to venture out. If you like live jazz and blues, the tiny **Cotton Club (19)** *(666 W. 125th St. at Riverside Drive,*

212-663-7890, www.cottonclub-newyork.com) has a great in-house band and offers dining and cocktails as well as brunch specials. (Note this isn't the original 1923 Cotton Club, but a newer venture established in 1978.) The **Lenox Lounge (20)** *(288 Malcolm X Blvd., W. 124th/W. 125th Sts., 212-427-0253, www.lenoxlounge. com),* however, is still in its original location, and its Deco décor and live jazz can waft you back on a serious time trip. **Showman's Bar (21)** *(375 W. 125th St., St. Nicholas/Morningside Aves., 212-864-8941),* established in 1942, is one of Harlem's genuine jazz treasures; drinks are inexpensive and it's all about the music here. **St. Nick's Pub (22)** *(773 St. Nicholas Ave. at W. 149th St., 212-283-9728)* is a crammed-full space that offers live jazz for a very reasonable cover (plus free soul food), and a chance every Monday to hear the excellent Sugar Hill Jazz Quartet work out.

WHERE TO SHOP

Money has come to Harlem in a big way recently, and although this has had a very obvious beneficial effect, it's also burdened Harlem with some of the more soulless commercial glitz of downtown, such as the vast Harlem USA Mall (23) *(300 W. 125th St., Adam Clayton Powell Jr./Frederick Douglass Blvds.),* though if you want the latest sneakers or street wear it comes in handy. For more personal stores check out the open-air Malcolm Shabazz Harlem Market (24) *(52 W. 116th St. at Malcolm X Blvd., 212-987-8131),* which sells wonderful African fabrics, clothes, and crafts. Want that Malcolm X or Martin Luther King, Jr. tee shirt that says you've been to

Harlem? These and many other Harlem-related items, including books and CDs, can be found at Soul Brothers Boutique (25) *(115 W. 128th St., Malcolm X/Adam Clayton Powell Jr. Blvds., 212-749-9005).*

When all this browsing makes you hungry, Settepani Bakery (26) *(196 Lenox Ave. at W. 120th St., 917-492-4806),* an Italian mini-chain, has mouthwatering pastries and breads to offer. In Spanish Harlem, the main shopping strip is along East 116th Street (27), which has become increasingly Mexican of late. There are plenty of small food vendors and stores known as botanicas, that sell candles and religious charms and icons. They're well worth visiting because botanicas are disappearing at a fast rate in the city as real estate developments roll over them.

WHERE TO STAY

Harlem has a number of relatively new bed-and-breakfasts, which are an intimate and easy way to get a feel for the neighborhood. The Harlem Landmark Guesthouse (28) ($$) *(437 W. 147th St. at Convent Ave., 212-694-8800)* is a fabulously restored town house that even offers a "honeymoon suite." The Harlem Flophouse (29) ($) *(242 W. 123rd St., Adam Clayton Powell Jr./Frederick Douglass Blvds., 212-662-0678)* is even more reasonably priced in another handsomely restored old building. There's a communal dining room and garden.

MORNINGSIDE HEIGHTS

B C *to Cathedral Parkway-110th St., 116th St., 125th St.;* **1** *to Cathedral Parkway-110th St., 116th St.-Columbia University, 125th St.*

● SNAPSHOT ●

Morningside Heights is "college town," thanks to its vast student and faculty population, including Columbia University and Barnard College, among many others. This makes it an ideal place to stroll while checking out the wonderful campus buildings and the inexpensive bars, cafes, and restaurants that cluster around them. The main shopping and eating drag is Broadway from 110th to 116th Streets, though there are many places tucked away in the side streets. Recently, the term "SoHa"—"South of Harlem"—has been applied to the neighborhood by real estate agents, an odious term but one that marks the notable trend for Upper West Siders to shift ever northwards in search of reasonably priced accommodation.

PLACES TO SEE
Landmarks:

The great landmark here—one of New York's finest—is the truly astonishing **Cathedral Church of St. John the Divine (30)** *(1047 Amsterdam Ave. at 112th St., 212-316-7540, www.stjohndivine.org).*

St. John's size has to be seen to be believed; it's bigger than Notre Dame and Chartres cathedrals in France combined, and the Statue of Liberty would fit beneath her dome. Even her famous Rose Window is the largest stained glass window in the country. St. John's was begun in 1892 and is still far from finished, as the empty niches on the exterior make clear. Teams of sculptors are still working on her today, and as a result the church represents a number of architectural styles. Tours of the grounds and interior are available. If you're here in October, don't miss the annual Blessing of the Animals as part of the Feast of St. Francis, when animals from horses and snakes to gerbils and rats parade up the aisle with their owners. The other major institution here is **Columbia University (31)** *(main entrance: Broadway at W. 114th St., 212-854-1254, www.columbia.edu)*, designed by Charles McKim of the famous architectural firm McKim, Mead & White in grand Beaux Arts style. The centerpiece is the **Low Memorial Library (32)**, a classical porticoed temple around which the other campus buildings are clustered. The campus is open to the public, though you need to be part of the regular student-led

tours to visit the interior elements. Visitors should head to the Visitors Center in the Low Library for information. **Morningside Park (33)** *(W. 110th/W. 123rd Sts., Morningside Ave./Morningside Drive, www.morningsidepark.org)* is a narrow band of parkway that separates Harlem from Morningside Heights. You really get a sense of the dramatic, rocky nature of Manhattan's topography here, before so much was flattened out for development. The views of St. John's are amazing.

PLACES TO EAT & DRINK
Where to Eat:

Kitchenette Uptown (34) ($) *(1272 Amsterdam Ave., W. 122nd/ W. 123rd Sts., 212-531-7600)* is a tiny spot and a favorite with college students and others on a tight budget who want succulent soul food and other south-

ern-fried delights. Next door there's **Max Soha (35) ($$)** *(1274 Amsterdam Ave. at W. 123rd St., 212-531-2221, cash only)*, serving can't-go-wrong Italian food at great prices, though its popularity means the lines can be long. If you don't mind shelling out some serious cash, **Terrace in the Sky (36) ($$$)** *(400 W. 119th St., Amsterdam Ave./Morningside Drive, 212-666-9490)* offers stunning views from its penthouse location. It serves terrific Mediterranean and French cuisine. On 110th Street there's the excellent **Bistro Ten 18 (56) ($$)** *(1018 Amsterdam Ave. at W. 110th St., 212-662-7600, www.bistroten18.com)* for simple well-produced American fare with a great view of the **Cathedral Church of St. John the Divine (30)**. The **Hungarian Pastry Shop (57) ($)** *(1030 Amsterdam Ave., W. 110th/W. 111th Sts., 212-866-4230)* is an Eastern European classic in the heart of college town. You can't beat its *sacher tortes* and *linzer tarts*, washed down with strong Viennese coffee.

Bars & Nightlife:

An amble down Broadway between about W. 110th and W. 116th streets reveals a large number of bars and cafes, all frequented by Columbia students and faculty. **Le Monde (37)** *(2885 Broadway, W. 112th/W. 113th Sts., 212-531-3939)* is a brasserie with good beer and atmosphere. The **Heights Bar and Grill (38)** *(2867 Broadway, W. 111th/W. 112th Sts., 212-866-7035)* has a (teensy) rooftop bar, and offers cheap Mexican food washed down with margaritas.

WHERE TO SHOP

Mondel Chocolates (39) *(2913 Broadway at W. 114th St., 212-865-2111)* has been going since 1943, and its old-fashioned vibe is the secret to its success. The Bank Street Bookstore (40) *(610 W. 112th St. at Broadway, 212-678-1654, www.bankstreetbooks.com),* is an excellent children's bookstore with a highly knowledgeable staff.

WASHINGTON HEIGHTS & INWOOD

WASHINGTON HEIGHTS: **C** *to 155th St., 163rd St.-Amsterdam Ave., 168th St.-Washington Heights;* **A** *to 168th St.-Washington Heights, 175th St., 181st St., 190th St., Dyckman St.;* **1** *to 157th St., 168th St., 181st St., 191st St., Dyckman St.*

INWOOD: **A** *to Inwood-207th St.;* **1** *to 207th St., 215th St.*

◈ SNAPSHOT ◈

Most New Yorkers live their entire lives never knowing what lies at Manhattan's northern tip. The answer is some of the best parks in the city, one of its best museums, great street life, and views of the Hudson River and of the New Jersey Palisades that can't be beat. It's definitely worth the trip. Washington Heights *(W. 155th/Dyckman (a.k.a. 200th) Sts., between the Hudson and Harlem Rivers)* and Inwood *(north of Dyckman St. between the Hudson and Harlem Rivers)* both used to be the sites of large estates and remained among the last parts of New York to be urbanized until the subway systems reached them in the 1930s. Washington Heights is home to one of the largest Dominican populations in the city, but its parks and handsome apartment buildings have

also become attractive recently to non-Hispanics, especially young artists, forced northwards by ever-escalating real estate prices. At its northern end is Fort Tryon Park, laid out by Frederick Law Olmsted (son of the Olmsted of Central Park fame), and home to the stunning Cloisters Museum, where the Metropolitan Museum maintains its medieval collection. Inwood has a relatively small residential population, and a beautiful park, Inwood Hill Park, where some of the last primeval forest in Manhattan can be found.

PLACES TO SEE
Landmarks:

The **George Washington Bridge (41)** *(spanning the Hudson River at 179th St.)*, one of New York's most amazing pieces of engineering (and lit up beautifully at night), can best be viewed from Fort Washington Avenue, which runs parallel to the waterfront. The virgin peaks on the far side, known as the Palisades, which are at their best in the fall, were bought up by the Rockefeller family to prevent development, perhaps the greatest of their many philanthropic acts. Washington Avenue eventually leads to **Fort Tryon Park (42)** *(W. 190th St. to Riverside Drive)*, a park that combines careful landscaping with the wild and rocky natural topography of the site. In the summer it's a favorite spot for weddings, and the views of both the city to the east and the Palisades across the river are breathtaking. The park is home to the **Cloisters Museum (43)** *(see "Arts & Entertainment," on page 185)*, a branch of The Metropolitan Museum of Art. **Inwood Hill Park (44)** *(north and west of Dyckman St. to the tip of Manhattan)* is the supposed site of original Dutch governor Peter Minuit's "purchase" of Manhattan from the Native American Lenapes in 1626, or so a plaque here will inform you. The park is densely filled in places with the last vestiges of the forest that once covered Manhattan from tip to tip. At the very northern end is the **Henry Hudson Bridge (45)**, and painted on the rocks nearby is the vast blue "C," for Columbia University, whose students play soccer and football at nearby Baker Field.

Arts & Entertainment:

The **Cloisters Museum (43)** *(Fort Washington Ave at Margaret Corbin Plaza, 212-923-3700, www.met museum.org)*, is a miracle of money and vision. In the 1930s the Rockefeller family, which owned the land that's now Fort Tryon Park, purchased, shipped back home, and reassembled elements of five medieval cloisters from Europe. The Met now houses its medieval art collection here, but the real attraction is this exquisite architectural sanctuary, perhaps the most peaceful spot in all of New York City. Another lovely museum in this neighborhood is the **Morris-Jumel Mansion (46)** *(65 Jumel Terrace, W. 160th/W. 162nd Sts., 212-923-8008)*, the oldest house in Manhattan and home to George Washington during parts of the Revolutionary War. It offers excellent tours of the house and grounds, as well as a number of children's programs.

PLACES TO EAT & DRINK
Where to Eat:
If you're visiting The Cloisters, the **New Leaf Café (47)** *(1 Margaret Corbin Drive near Park Drive, 212-568-5323, www.nyrp.org/newleaf)* is a great place to stop for a bite. There's also jazz in the evenings and a pleasant open-air terrace. In Washington Heights try **Bohio (48) ($$)** *(4055 Broadway, W. 170th/W. 171st Sts., 212-568-5029)* for really good Dominican food in a small but pleasant space. **DR-K (49) ($$)** *(114 Dyckman St. at Nagle Ave., 212-304-1717)* offers tasty "Nuevo Latino" dishes, particularly seafood, with great mojitos to wash it all down.

Bars & Nightlife:
Washington Heights has always had a buzzing street life at night, but with gentrification has come a hip bar scene. **Viva (50)** *(4168 Broadway, W. 176th/W. 177th Sts., 212-923-8700)* is a sleek bar/lounge that caters mostly, but not entirely, to a young and often well educated second-generation Dominican crowd. **The Monkey Room Bar (51)** *(589 Fort Washington Ave. at W. 187th St., 212-543-9888)* is a hip, eclectic spot that serves as a morning coffee shop as well as a DJ-heavy nightclub.

WHERE TO SHOP
It probably won't be the kind of couture you can pick up in the fancier nabes downtown, but at the Washington Heights branch of thrift store chain Goodwill Industries (52) *(514 W. 181st St. at Amsterdam*

Ave., 212-923-7910, www.goodwillny.org) you might find a genuine Guayaberas shirt that'll look cool in the local bars. The Met has one of the best gift shops of all museums, and its branch at the Cloisters, **Cloisters Gift Shop (43)** *(see Cloisters Museum in "Arts & Entertainment," on page 185)* has plenty of fun medieval kitsch to take home as a memento.

INDEX